感 謝 状

セント・ポールズ校殿

貴校は昭和二十四年以来成蹊高等学校との間で活発な教育交流計画を実施され日米間の相互理解の促進に大きな役割を果されました
このたび本計画開始三十五周年を迎えるにあたり日米間の友好親善関係強化の為に果された貴校の多年に亘るご努力とご貢献に対し深く感謝の意を表します

昭和五十九年八月十五日

日本国外務大臣

A Generous Idea

A Generous Idea

St. Paul's School and Seikei Gakuen

David T. Dana III

POSTERITY
PRESS

On the Cover
*[background] The Old Chapel at St. Paul's School, consecrated in
1859—a pencil drawing by Takahiro Hiraoka, who in 1985 became
the first Japanese academic to teach at St. Paul's.
[insert] The Yukimidooroo—a lantern to light a snow covered path—
the gift to St. Paul's School from the first eleven Seikei scholars.*

Endpapers
*Letter of appreciation in two languages from the Foreign Minister of
Japan to St. Paul's School on the 35th anniversary of the exchange
program with Seikei Gakuen that began in 1949.*

At right
*St. Paul's School's first three Seikei scholars stand together in 1954:
Tatsuo Arima, then a freshman at Harvard; Minoru 'Ben' Makihara, a
senior at Harvard; and Yoshiaki Shimizu, a fifth former at St. Paul's.*

Posterity Press, Inc.
PO Box 71081
Chevy Chase, Maryland 20813

© 2000 St. Paul's School
All rights reserved. Printed in the United States of America

Library of Congress Cataloging-in-Publication Data
Dana, David T.
    A generous idea : St. Paul's School and Seikei Gakuen/David T. Dana.
      p. cm.
    Includes bibliographical references.
    ISBN 1-889274-13-5 (pbk. : alk. paper)
    1. Student exchange programs—New Hampshire—Concord—
History—Case studies. 2. Student exchange programs—Japan—
Tokyo—History—Case studies. 3. St. Paul's School (Concord, N.H.)
—History. 4. Seikei Gakuen—History. I. Title: St. Paul's School and
Seikei Gakuen. II. Title.

LB2376.3.J3 D25 2000
373'.01'1620952135—dc21   00-031375
                                                                                             CIP

Contents

Foreword 7

Acknowledgments 10

Chapter 1   'The Happiest Period'—The Beginning   15
Chapter 2   'We Wish To Continue'—The First Decade   29
Chapter 3   'Rich And Rewarding'—The Sixties And Seventies   45
Chapter 4   'Even More Interesting'—The Eighties   59
Chapter 5   'On The Heels Of A Typhoon'—The Americans In Japan   79
Chapter 6   'Ringing Loud'—The Advanced Studies Program   95
Chapter 7   'In Honor Of Those'—The Nineties   107
Chapter 8   'How Great The Rewards'—The Graduates   117

Epilogue 132
Notes 135
Bibliography 143
Appendices
    Appendix A, Hugh Camp Cup Prize Speech   147
    Appendix B, Japanese Students At St. Paul's   149
    Appendix C, American Students At Seikei   150
    Appendix D, Visiting Japanese Teachers   151
    Appendix E, St. Paul's-Seikei Prize Recipients   152
    Appendix F, SPS Award Recipients   152

St. Paul's School students and teachers head for class after assembly in the Chapel of St. Peter and St. Paul, in 1999.

Foreword

What changes in the life of St. Paul's School do you intend to introduce this year?" A concerned mother of a new student had directed this question to Henry C. Kittredge, sixth rector of St. Paul's School.

It was September 1949.

The answer Mr. Kittredge gave was characteristically informative, humorous, and somewhat blunt: "None. I do not plan to introduce any changes this year because I expect it will take all of my energies and time just to respond to the changes that will be forced upon me by students, faculty, and alumni."

Did this really happen? I have heard Mr. Kittredge tell this story about himself many times, so I am sure the meaning conveyed is accurate. Henry Kittredge saw himself as the conservator of a fine educational institution, not as a revolutionary reformer.

How, then, could this amiable schoolmaster have been responsible for initiating a program destined to exert great influence throughout the cultural and political life of two great countries, the United States and Japan? For that, surely, is what has happened as a consequence of the decision by Mr. Kittredge to admit one student from Seikei School of Tokyo to the Sixth Form of St. Paul's School, in September 1949, four years after the end of World War II.

One recalls large-scale activities underway in 1949. In Europe, through the Marshall Plan, the United States was busy helping reconstruct buildings, bridges, and infrastructure so recently destroyed, and mending the shattered lives of people everywhere. Most importantly, this nation was planting and tending seeds for the growth of democratic, free-market societies.

In Asia, after widespread destruction, the United States was engaged first in helping the Japanese achieve the necessities of daily life, then in fostering the development of business activities necessary for a strong, modern state. Through the forceful efforts of General Douglas MacArthur, America was emphasizing the principles of modern democracy. This was the work of an idealistic people.

It is perhaps no wonder, then, that in one small corner of the United States, at St. Paul's School in Concord, New Hampshire, a decision based on hope and trust in the future would be taken.

Mr. Kittredge did not initiate important change? Oh yes he did. In this one small step, the admission of one young man from Tokyo, probably without realizing it, he set loose forces that would gain momentum and power over the following 50 years, as friendships and ambitions and respect and affection multiplied, producing what is now known as the Seikei-St. Paul's partnership.

In writing *A Generous Idea* David T. Dana SPS '55 has told the story of a remarkable cooperative achievement, from small beginnings to the present era of substantial influence. As a student in St. Paul's School, from September 1950 through graduation in 1955, Mr. Dana knew the second Seikei student. The third Seikei scholar was his classmate and friend. Having watched the developments through these 50 years with keen interest, he is an authoritative voice in their telling. Graduates of the two schools and concerned members of the government, business, and cultural communities of both countries will be grateful for this book and will be caught up in the fascinating details of these relationships so clearly related.

Mr. Kittredge believed he was not an initiator of change. In what a positive and wonderful sense he was wrong! The heroic courage of the Seikei students in coming to an unknown land, and the heroic courage of students and faculty in so warmly receiving them, produce a powerful story.

Our two countries and our world are much the better for it. The lessons Mr. Dana highlights could well be applied among many people in the world today.

William A. Oates
Rector Emeritus
St. Paul's School

The Seikei School motto, "Peaches and plums utter no words, yet underneath will form a beaten path," adorns a scroll brushed by the calligrapher Shinzan Kamijo. Hanging in SPS's Ohrstrom Library the scroll was given by Seikei alumni and teachers in 1978.

Foreword

Acknowledgments

When my classmate Yoshiaki Shimizu asked me to help celebrate the St. Paul's-Seikei 50th anniversary, I offered to write a history of the exchange program. When I made that offer, I had not given any consideration to what kind of history it would be. I suppose I pictured a historical narrative filled with facts, statistics, dates, and procedures like most histories I had read. I wanted to find out how a relationship between a preparatory school in a rural New Hampshire hamlet and one in a metropolitan Japanese capitol began, how it grew, what supported it, how problems were overcome along the way, and what was accomplished.

The Japanese have an apt word, *shoshin*. It means "an empty mind." It does not mean "stupid" or "empty headed"; rather, it is complimentary: a "beginner's mind" ready to be filled, to accept new ideas, open to anything. An ideal student has *shoshin*. I had *shoshin*. However, bit by bit, as I learned more and more about the program, a concept for the history revealed itself.

This was not to be a history of the schools. Institutions can create opportunities and St. Paul's and Seikei certainly did, but individuals take the opportunities and make things happen. This is a story of people, not of facts, statistics, or procedures. It is a story about remarkable people of two nations—farsighted educators and courageous young men and women—all highly intelligent, perceptive, articulate scholars. This history is their story. It had to be told in their words as much as possible.

Many people did research and writing for this history. Foremost I must thank André O. Hurtgen. The recently retired St. Paul's teacher, former head of the Modern Languages Department, and for many years a mentor to students in the Seikei connection, was my indispensable presence at SPS. Because I live in California, I could not investigate the school's archives. André did that for me, carrying out every request with enthusiasm and thoroughness. He spent hours poring over old SPS publications, yearbooks, minutes, and files. He hounded the SPS administrative staff. He supervised mailing my questions to Seikei alumni and teachers. His suggestions and advice saved me from mistakes. And he compiled information, sending me numerous e-mail messages, photocopies, letters, and photographs. And, of course, his recollections and writings added immeasurable detail and color. Thank you, André.

SPS Rector Craig Anderson and Vice Rector Sharon D. Hennessey gave their support to the project. They made it possible for members of the school staff to take time from regular duties to respond to my requests. Benjamin R. Neilson, chairman of the St. Paul's School Board of Trustees, smoothed the way to research in the trustees' minutes.

Members of the St. Paul's administrative staff helped. Joan C. Smith of the Alumni Office coordinated mailing, receiving, and forwarding questionnaires. Bob Rettew, director of Information Systems, and David Levesque, librarian, gathered information from the Ohrstrom Library archives. Dr. J. C. Douglas Marshall, dean of faculty, Robert W. Hill III, associate dean of faculty, and Donna M. Bowe, their assistant, gathered material about SPS faculty. Nicole C. Springer, Joan Smith and Debbie Tattersall of the Alumni Office prepared and sent questionnaires and helped find facts on alumni. Jeffrey Bradley, director of the Advanced Studies Program (ASP), and Joyce Ashcroft, his secretary, collected ASP student statements and advised about the ASP program. Michael R. Barwell, director, Cindy Foote, and Mary Ann Murphy in the Communications department collected photographs.

In Japan, Professor Mamoru Shimizu, former Seikei principal, copied and sent his entire file of correspondence from the 1950s — the early correspondence between SPS and Seikei. Satoru Nakajima, Seikei's coordinator of Exchange Programs for many years, answered questions and sent much important information. He selected photographs of SPS students in Japan and of school scenes. His recollections, descriptions, and stories were invaluable. Makoto Tokutomi also provided photographs.

Yoshiaki Shimizu started me on this project. To him I owe thanks for introductions, recollections, photos, and hours of conversation; for advice on Japanese language, manners, and customs; for correcting mistakes and offering thoughtful analysis.

William A. Oates, eighth SPS rector and now rector emeritus, spent hours looking in his files and sent me many documents, photos, articles, and letters. I could not have done without his recollections, passed on through letters, telephone conversations, and a delightful time at his home in Kennebunkport, Maine.

The Most Reverend Frank T. Griswold, presiding bishop of the Episcopal Church USA; Jennifer Peters, assistant archivist for reference and public service, Episcopal Church Archives; and Rev. Samuel I. Koshiishi, general secretary, Nippon Sei Ko Kai, all helped track down information from their respective archives. Maygene Daniels, chief archivist at the National Gallery of Art, furnished information.

I am grateful to all the program graduates who replied to my written questions. Whether or not I used quotations or information from them, their recollections gave me the flavor of student experiences and painted a total picture of the program, for there were responses about every decade of the 50 years. The Japanese graduates were Minoru Makihara '50, Tatsuo Arima '53, Hachiro Nakamura '61, Yoshiharu Akabane '63, Matsumi Kikyo '71, Kaoru Yamauchi '75, Amy Yoshiko Nobu '78, Hiroko Yamashita Teratani '81, Akiko Higaki '84, Miki Tanaka '84, Yoko Nishikawa '90, Michiyuki Nagasawa '91, Hana Sugimoto '92, Leon Ochiai '94, Kiyoshi Ayako Kubota '97, and Shunsuke Okano '97.

The American graduates who sent answers were Loring R. McAlpin '78, Elisabeth Bentel Carpenter '83, Charles Dunn McKee, Jr. '83, Tara McGowan Okada '84, Craig D. Sherman '85, Joshua H. Brooks '86, Caroline Kenney '91, Julian J. Wimbush '91, and Timothy Cooke Ferriss '95.

These Seikei teachers who traveled to SPS for one or two weeks to participate in the Advanced Studies Program also provided recollections of their experiences: Sayaka Atobe, Takahiro Hiraoka, Hisao Minami, Satoru Nakajima, Koichi Nihei, Hiromi Takahashi, Tadaaki Shimizu, and Michiko Yamato.

These ASP students sent recollections after Jeffrey Bradley contacted them for me: Crystal Brunelli, Katy Clark, Charo D'Etcheverry, Abigail Dunne, Kara French, Joshua Hornik, Jason Kidd, Juliana Mastronunzio, Jessica McDermott, Shireen Meskoob, Mary Mulcahey, Kristen Ray, and Kristen Schade.

People who gave more extensive oral or written interviews, or both, were André Hurtgen, Yoshiaki Shimizu, Mamoru Shimizu, William A. Oates, Satoru Nakajima, Richard Okada, Frank T. Griswold, Kathleen Zimpfer, Jeff Bradley, Masatoshi Shimano, Alan Hall, Robert A. G. Monks, and H. Douglas Barklay.

Many of the students and teachers who replied to the questionnaires sent personal photographs. André Hurtgen, Yoshiaki Shimizu, and William Oates also furnished pictures never before published. Seikei and St. Paul's supplied campus scenes and archival photographs.

William A. Oates, André Hurtgen, and Yoshiaki Shimizu reviewed a draft manuscript. Their attention to detail, knowledge of facts, and experience correcting papers saved me from mistakes in both fact and grammar.

This history project could not have happened without the support of all these many alumni, teachers, and administrators. I thank them all.

Finally, my editor, Philip Kopper, contributed a sense for the right word, attention to detail and perceptive suggestions, all of which added color, interest and completeness. Importantly, he provided a perspective to the story independent of those personally involved. For all that, and his friendship, I owe him many thanks.

I have tried to tell stories and record accurately the important events that took place over 50 years. If there are errors of any kind, whether in judgments, facts, interpretations, or quotations, the responsibility is mine alone.

D.T.D.

New Hampshire's rich woodlands surround the chapels, libraries, rectory and schoolhouse—landmark buildings of St. Paul's School—between the athletic fields and the Lower Pond where generations of students have skated and rowed.

CHAPTER 1

'The Happiest Period'
The Beginning

Since 1856 well-to-do families of Boston, New York, and Philadelphia have sent their sons to the New Hampshire woods near Concord for the nine-month school year at St. Paul's School. At this traditional New England preparatory school the boys lived in an idyllic country world of trees, fields, and ponds. In 1856 Henry Augustus Coit, a 24-year-old schoolmaster, with his bride and three students had started St. Paul's School in the country home of a Boston doctor, George C. Shattuck. There Coit taught Shattuck's sons and shaped the school's values—based in Christian faith amid natural beauty. Coit chose the school motto: *Ea discamus in terris quorum scientia perseveret in coelis*: "Let us learn those things on earth the knowledge of which continues in heaven." Thereafter St. Paul's School acquired some attributes of an English boarding school and grew into one of the nation's premier private schools.

In 1923 Rector Samuel Drury wanted St. Paul's School to "open the door and step forward" to produce "not only good Americans, but good citizens of the world." He pictured raising money for ten scholarships for students from Europe and Asia, but the trustees voted down any scholarships for foreign boys. About ten years later,

Warren Hall—a pencil sketch by Takahiro Hiraoka, who visited SPS in 1985 to teach Japanese culture in the Advanced Studies Program.

scholarships were approved for English boys only and a few attended. SPS remained a school that prepared American boys from the northeastern United States for college.

At the end of World War II, St. Paul's enrolled about 450 boys aged 12 to 18. Teachers, called "masters," taught, coached, and mentored the boys, who were organized into six "forms," corresponding to grades seven through twelve. Graduating seniors were "Sixth Formers." For the most part, they studied required courses in science, math, sacred studies, English, and American and European literature and history in a great schoolhouse. They lived in dormitories and ate in vast dining halls scattered in the woods. Latin, Greek, French, a little Spanish, and German were taught. Every day and twice on Sunday the boys filed in and out of a soaring gothic chapel for Episcopal services. All students wore neckties to class and blue suits to Sunday chapel.

Even the most bookish student participated in athletics. The most popular sports were football, hockey, and crew, but other sports abounded, too—track, wrestling, gymnastics, baseball, basketball, squash, skiing, tennis, and soccer. No one was to question a master acting as referee or umpire, and both winners and losers cheered and told each other, "Good game," after each contest. Every Sunday after-

Henry Crocker Kittredge, sixth rector, began the Seikei program.

noon boys searched for the master whose wife served the tastiest cookies at tea. Over all this presided a head master, known as the rector. A board of trustees supervised the school's endowment and set the budget with which the rector operated, preparing the boys to enter the country's elite colleges. In the years before World War II, Harvard, Yale, and Princeton had accepted 80 to 90 percent of St. Paul's graduates.

In the spring of 1948 Henry Crocker Kittredge had completed his first year as the sixth rector of St. Paul's School, although he preferred to teach. For nearly 40 years SPS boys had received his teaching—a gentle, but firm prodding into independent and original thinking. Kittredge knew boys well. He had not wanted to be rector.

The first rector who was not an ordained minister, Kittredge had been brought up in the puritan values of New England. He personified the traditional wisdom expected of a Christian educator. This New England icon with bobbing eyebrows presided over a school secluded, peaceful, and steeped in a traditional curriculum.

But great events were shaking the world in 1948. Just three years previously, American and Soviet troops had rolled up Hitler's Reich, and the American bomber *Enola Gay* ended World War II in a mushroom cloud of destruction over Japan. Much of Europe and Asia lay ruined. The United States was providing enormous economic aid to rebuild Europe under the Marshall Plan. The Soviet Union had installed puppet governments in Eastern Europe and threatened the same for Greece, Turkey, and Iran. A massive and dangerous American and British airlift supplied Soviet-blockaded Berlin, and Communists took over Czechoslovakia. In China, Mao Tse-tung's Communist insurgents had chased Chiang Kai-shek's Nationalist government to the island of Taiwan and controlled the mainland. The United States, having sustained almost no physical damage in the world war, was the only nation that had the economic strength to confront the poverty, disease, and destruction so widespread elsewhere. It was the only democratic nation with the military and diplomatic clout to effectively oppose the expansionist Soviet Union and dictatorial Communism.

American forces occupied defeated Japan. American troops, economists, educators, and technicians were reorganizing the shocked and destitute society into a more democratic model. In the United States, American families were rebuilding their disrupted lives and creating economic prosperity. At the start of the war the government had interned thousands of persons of Japanese descent in concentration camps. These Japanese-American families, too, were rebuilding their lives, but racism and biases against Asian stereotypes existed within the American populace.

Such were the forces and sentiments abroad in the land when Henry Kittredge concluded his first year as rector of the old school tucked away in rural New Hampshire. In addition to teaching scholarship, sportsmanship, honor, and reverence, he saw that St. Paul's must teach some of the nation's brightest students to understand the international stage onto which their country had been thrust. Kittredge, working in the old Victorian frame mansion at the campus center, reflected on the momentous international events that were taking place. What implications did all this have for 450 intelligent boys?

He could not really know, but implications there were sure to be. He wrote to the St. Paul's School trustees: "It is hard enough for adults to keep abreast of national and foreign affairs or to interpret them accurately in times which, like our own, are bewilderingly unstable and infinitely complex. It is harder still for the boys. Yet because our country has become a mighty factor in international relations, and will inevitably continue to be one, it is increasingly important for boys to be given some idea of the principal elements in the picture and some notion of the new responsibility that rests on every American."

Now that America was a "mighty factor" in international affairs, "principal elements" in an American boy's education had to expose him to cultural differences and ways of foreign thinking. How to carry out this conviction? In 1949, at the end of his second year as rector, Kittredge again wrote the trustees:

"The geographical distribution of our boys is still too narrow...whether or not we succeed in persuading one or two of our

Upper Formers to take a year abroad, we should certainly open our doors to qualified boys from abroad, and let them know we have done so. At no time in the world's history has such an invitation been more necessary. If the School is to do its duty in preparing American boys for the kind of life into which they will emerge, we must give them every opportunity to associate at close range and for considerable periods of time with boys of other nationalities. If our school is to live, it cannot remain in a sort of rarified isolation any more than our Nation can."

Occasionally in the past the school had taken in students from England, Europe, or South America. These boys, of wealthy parentage, entered on the same paying basis as American students. They usually had lived in or had earlier schooling in the United States, spoke English well, and were nearly as American as other students. The idea Kittredge conceived would require more—of both the student and the school.

Kittredge recently had hired an assistant chaplain and teacher, the Reverend David McAlpin Pyle. Before the war, the tall, slightly built Pyle had been personal secretary to Joseph Grew, the American ambassador to Japan. In Tokyo, Pyle had made friends among American and Japanese Christians and had come to love the Japanese people. The war forced him back to the United States where he was ordained in the Episcopal Church. He joined the SPS sacred studies department in 1948, and SPS boys promptly dubbed the quiet, thoughtful, cleric "Pious Pyle."

David McAlpin Pyle, the SPS teacher who had lived in Japan before World War II.

Pyle's affection for the Japanese people had not left him. Personal agony over the wartime wrongs the two countries had done each other led him to seek some small step that could help in reconciling the people and healing the wounds. He believed that international understand-

"The Happiest Period"

ing could be improved through personal relationships and that the most promising of all relationships are those that develop during school days.

When he learned of Kittredge's desire to expose St. Paul's School students to foreign contacts, Pyle jumped at the chance to help both Japan and his new school. He suggested that a Japanese student come to St. Paul's on a scholarship each year or two. Rector Kittredge gave his full support: "See what you can do."

With this essential encouragement from Kittredge, Pyle turned to friends from pre-war days in Tokyo. One of those friends was the Reverend Kenneth Leslie Abbott Viall, a Harvard graduate and a missionary in the Society of St. John the Evangelist. This organization of Christian missionaries based nearby in Cambridge, Massachusetts, knew St. Paul's well, and the Episcopalian clergy at SPS had had personal contacts there for over 75 years. Viall would help St. Paul's.

When Pyle knew him in the late 1930s, Viall had been pursuing missionary work as an English instructor in Japan at Rikkyo (St. Paul's) University and as a chaplain at the Holy Trinity American Church, Tokyo. After spending the war years in the United States, Viall had returned to Japan to represent the National Council to the Anglican Church in Japan. Pyle wrote to his friend: Did he by any chance know of a Japanese boy who wanted to study in the United States?

In Japan in 1948, some 83 million shocked and demoralized people barely survived in a land flattened by bombing and weakened by the excesses of war. Firebombs had destroyed 60 percent of Tokyo. Half of Japan's cities were in ruins. Food was scarce.

Promptly after the formal surrender, the Supreme Allied Commander, General Douglas MacArthur, had set about remaking Japanese society in the American image. The Emperor had renounced his divinity. The United States furnished food, clothing, and medicines. With American help, the demilitarized Japanese reformed landholdings and set up a representative government with a new constitution. The great *zaibatsu* (industrial conglomerates), such as Mitsubishi, were dismantled and reformed as smaller, independent companies.

A 15-year-old schoolboy, writing a few years later, recalled what it was like: "Our class had been evacuated from Tokyo at the beginning of July when the air raids had become really severe, and since then we had been up here digging the hard and untouched ground to plant sweet potatoes and vegetables.... The rows of boys, fifteen years old, stripped to their waists, their bony backs shining with sweat, steadily advanced day by day. Cutting grass with those small sickles was hard, too. Every time you stood up to stretch yourself, you would feel dizzy.... We did not know for what we were working but we knew that we had to work. But now, the war being over, that feeling was gone.... A small tin of condensed milk, that was enough for twenty boys. Just a lick for each of them, and then everybody was happy.... Now we had hope to go back to our homes but we felt so miserable. We were like stray puppies whimpering and whining."

That schoolboy was Minoru Makihara. Minoru's father, an executive with Mitsubishi, had lived in London with his young family in the 1930s. There Minoru had grown up and learned English. When the war broke out, Mr. Makihara was detained, and Minoru and his mother returned to Tokyo. Later Minoru's father was exchanged for an English businessman, and he joined his country's war effort. In 1942 Mr. Makihara was named to head a joint Mitsubishi-Mitsui reconstruction project in the Philippines. When a U.S. submarine torpedoed his ship on the way to Manila, he was killed. As the war ended, Minoru, like thousands of other Japanese, was living in a tent near Tokyo, from which his mother walked 45 miles to bring food. Minoru soon returned to school at the fine, private, Mitsubishi-supported Seikei Gakuen.

The first: Minoru 'Ben' Makihara, 1950.

Seikei (pronounced "Say-kay") had been founded as a business school in 1912 by Haruji Nakamura, who had learned about English public schools and modeled Seikei similarly, with students in dormitories some of which resembled English Victorian houses. He believed education should develop individual potential and character, not rote learning. The name Seikei, "the forming of a path," is derived from an ancient Chinese proverb 桃李不言下自成蹊 "peaches and plums utter no words, yet underneath will form a beaten path." The beautiful blossoms and sweet fruit of peaches and plums naturally attract

"The Happiest Period"

people and soon a beaten path to them forms. Here, the peaches and plums symbolize the man of character who, without vaunting himself, attracts people by the strength of his virtuous deeds. Such a man wins admiration even in his silence. Nakamura had selected the name Seikei to describe the ideally educated man.

By 1925, the Seikei School had become a full educational institution from elementary through high school and university levels. Students no longer lived on campus. Nakamura's educational philosophy had continued. The school's campus was on the outskirts of Tokyo, surrounded by fields and trees.

Before World War II, Seikei was an elite Japanese private institution, largely supported by the Mitsubishi *zaibatsu*. War destroyed the school's financial base but national educational reforms by the Allies enabled the school to continue with a larger student body, while installing schedules and procedures similar to those of schools in the United States. Seikei could no longer afford only a small number of elite students so its enrollment had been increased with paying students. Nine years were compulsory for all youth, male and female. New colleges and universities had to be created to accommodate the added students and there were serious shortages of teachers, classrooms, and books.

Minoru Makihara returned to a changed and reforming place, still one of Japan's best private schools. In 1949, about 1,500 boys and girls attended the high school, gathering every day in neat rows for morning assemblies, wearing dark blue uniforms, bowing when the *sensei* (teacher) entered, respectfully listening while the *sensei* lectured. Science, math, ancient Japanese history, modern history, calligraphy, Japanese literature, and English were among the subjects in a twelve-course load the high school students carried. They studied hard, prepared for exams, and learned to conform to the rules of Japanese behavior. The athletically inclined enjoyed traditional martial arts, tennis, and soccer. Seikei high school graduates did exceptionally well in the college exams, and in interscholastic academic contests like public speaking, music, and dance.

Makihara's English teacher at Seikei and its former principal, Professor Mamoru Shimizu, remembers him as a "quiet boy" who did not show off his fine pronunciation of English. In 1947, Seikei was invited to a national intercollegiate oratorical contest for the MacArthur Trophy, sponsored by the *Mainichi Shimbun*, Japan's second largest national newspaper. Professor Shimizu asked Makihara if he intended to enter. He "agreed on the spot." Makihara was perhaps the youngest contestant and, much to Professor Shimizu's amazement, he won. The following year he won first prize again! Minoru Makihara had become one of the most distinguished students in Japan.

The Japanese had learned to learn from foreigners. Nearly a century earlier, the Meiji emperor had proclaimed: "Knowledge shall be sought all over the world so as to strengthen the foundations of imperial rule." Minoru Makihara had accomplished all he could in Japan's schools, and he wanted to go to Harvard.

The Makihara family had joined the Anglican Church in London. Having returned to Japan when war broke out, they had frequented the Anglican Holy Trinity American Church in Tokyo, and there met the Reverend Kenneth Leslie Abbott Viall. He had left Japan during the war, but returned to Tokyo and the Anglican Church in Japan in 1947. Mrs. Makihara and her distinguished only son renewed their acquaintance with him and a friendship developed.

In 1949 Viall received a letter from his friend, David Pyle, the teacher at St. Paul's School. Did he by any chance know a Japanese student who might want to study in America? The Bishop knew that Makihara dreamed of studying at Harvard. A Harvard graduate himself, Viall realized that entrance into Harvard would require more preparation and academic credentials than Makihara had. St. Paul's School, with its excellent record in preparing boys for Ivy League colleges, would be a perfect stepping-stone for the ambitious young scholar. It was easy to recommend the outstanding Minoru Makihara to St. Paul's.

St. Paul's accepted Makihara readily and agreed to provide his tuition and living expenses. He would, however, have to get to Concord on his own. It is not known who paid Makihara's travel expenses, though Makihara credits Viall as the one "who brought me here." Taking with him only $30 in cash, the maximum that could be taken out of Japan, he depended on the goodwill of a freighter captain to see him safely halfway around the world.

In June 1949 Makihara said goodbye to his tearful mother. "Sometime before Makihara-kun went on his pioneering journey from Yokohama," reported Professor Shimizu, "we had a farewell tea party on his behalf in one of the rooms of the old library. Bishop Viall was also invited. In his greetings to the departing student, the Bishop remarked in his usual quiet and thoughtful tone that Mrs. Makihara was indeed a "brave woman to let him go!" Seikei Trustee Emeritus Kikuzo Tanioka recalls: "Not knowing what was in store for him in the victor country, we sent him off in trepidation—would he not be made a target of discrimination and bullying?"

A small crowd of teachers and friends from Seikei gathered at the Yokohama docks to see Makihara sail and wish him good fortune. The 18-year-old scholar and prize-winning English linguist, no doubt seized by some anxiety, boarded a slow Japanese freighter. He walked purposefully up the gangway and handed his ticket to the captain. It was a one-way ticket.

For over three weeks, the ship tossed and rolled across the Pacific. It took him through the Panama Canal in tropical July heat, chugged east through the Caribbean Sea, passed the Florida Keys, then turned north and for more long weeks steamed up the East Coast of the United States to New York. Makihara found a train to Boston and changed for Concord. The journey from Yokohama to Concord had lasted nearly two months. It would be five years before he saw his homeland again.

"When I arrived here in 1949, Japanese were still a rarity after the war, but I was received with an extraordinary warm welcome from the entire school." Vice-Rector Franklin V. Lloyd, Jr., gave him scholastic guidance. Makihara wondered what to do about buying books, paper, pencils, and supplies. "But, shortly after my arrival, I was given a checkbook of the school and was told that 'if you do need something you just have to write a check,' and so I did so without knowing how such expenses would be covered." He reported to Seikei that he been received at SPS with "great kindness."

Makihara immediately immersed himself in St. Paul's School life. He lived in the cavernous New Upper with an American roommate, Chauncey F. Dewey. Typically for teenaged boarding school boys, Makihara acquired a nickname. Years before, he had been baptized in England with the Christian name Bernard. At SPS he became "Ben." He was assigned to the intramural athletic clubs, the Delphian Club and the Shattuck Rowing Club. "A few of us tried to make sure

Before class, Makihara and formmates await a master's arrival.

he had enough money and a place to go during vacations," classmate Robert Monks remembers. Monks says that on a vacation with him during a school break, "We were stopped by a policeman in Gettysburg who admired Ben's original approach to driving."

Makihara spoke English with a slight London accent. He modestly described his command of English as "fairly good" when he arrived. SPS improved it, he said, "particularly in writing abilities." Pushing himself to improve further, Makihara joined the Cadmean Literary Society where he honed his public speaking skills and practiced the art of formal debating. At the student-run *Horae Scholasticae* he reviewed and selected stories, poems, and essays for publication. He wrote two touching stories of his experiences in postwar Japan. "The Hen," Makihara's fictional account of a student's return to a country village where the only hen was killed for meat to honor his visit, won the *Horae* literary prize.

Makihara studied his host country. J. Carroll McDonald's American history class stimulated him in valuable ways. Like all students, he took the required sacred studies course. He joined the

Acolyte Guild and the Scientific Society. A yearbook photograph shows Makihara in class as sharply and cleanly shined and clothed in jacket and tie as the most preppy of American boys around him.

One evening, standing before most of the school faculty, administration, and student body, Minoru Ben Makihara, 18-year-old foreign exchange student, delivered the prize speech in the Hugh Camp Cup Competition (see the Appendix). His words are remembered 50 years later. With that single short speech, Makihara set a standard to which all future Japanese students would aspire. The first student from Seikei voiced as no one else ever has the guiding theme that Kittredge and Pyle and the SPS faculty started when they invited him to enroll.

He started with a thought-provoking twist on the Declaration of Independence, "All men are created equal, but they are not the same." Then Makihara made his audience bluntly aware of simple and great differences between American and Japanese cultures. Standing before the school in pressed dark blue suit and necktie, he evoked an indelible image. "If I were now in Japan…I would be wearing a black cape and a torn black cap; I would be wearing wooden clogs instead of these shoes; and I would have a filthy towel dangling from my belt." (This was not a sign of poverty; rather this costume symbolized rugged humility and, paradoxically, was an expression of elegance. At the time, it was a common uniform in which rich and poor students could feel comfortable.)

Outward appearances were one thing, deep patterns of thought were another. "As a result of their long contact with Asiatic mysticism and Buddhism, Japanese students have a great affinity for philosophy…. They like to think in abstract terms, and so there is a tendency among the students to show externally that they do not care about material things. Thus we see that a Japanese student would have a different way of thinking compared with you, the boys of St. Paul's School."

Makihara's speech formed a path to the future. Reminding everyone with vivid examples from current world affairs that the habits of one culture are not necessarily the best for another, the distinguished young man from a devastated Japan concluded, "I believe that from among the boys of this school we shall see diplomats, politicians, and statesmen appear, and I believe that all of you will become active members of this democratic society. Therefore I ask you again, please try to understand the different backgrounds of different nations.... If you are unable to collect facts, select them, and interpret them correctly, it is as bad as being prejudiced. You may accept the fact that a Japanese student looks different, but if you cannot look beyond his appearance and realize its significance, your acceptance of it is meaningless.... All men are created equal, but they are not the same."

Makihara stayed at SPS one year. "On the eve of our graduation, I was invited to come to the rectory, which at the time was a rather remote and closed edifice. On meeting with Mr. Kittredge, I thanked him for the wonderful year spent at SPS. With a twinkle in his eye, he replied that he had enjoyed my presence, that all my expenses had been covered, and that he was going to give me a small gift. He handed me an envelope. The envelope contained a check, which I believe was about $400. I returned to the rectory the next day and thanked Mr. Kittredge. He asked me whether I knew of Robin Hood. I replied 'Yes, sir.' He said, again with a twinkle in his eye, 'Robin Hood was a robber. He stole from people who could afford to be robbed, and gave away his loot to people he liked. Never thank a robber!'"

Makihara graduated *magna cum laude*. He had proved a distinguished scholar in the United States, too, and he had thrived in personal ways. As the Robin Hood story attests, he vividly remembers Kittredge's wit and kindness. Years later, during his successful business career, Makihara said, "Although I stayed at SPS only for one year, it was one of the happiest periods in my life, and I was fortunate enough to develop lasting, valuable friendships which have bound me to SPS...and which have guided me in my professional life and provided me solace in moments of anxiety."

Harvard accepted Makihara in 1950 on a full scholarship. He earned an additional $50 for his Harvard expenses that summer as a counselor at Timberlake Camp, a Quaker boys camp in Woodstock, Vermont, and entered Harvard in the fall. He had realized his dream, and St. Paul's had exposed its students and faculty to their first friend from Japan.

Why Japanese Wanted to Go to St. Paul's

Japanese students have expressed a wonderful variety of reasons for going half way around the world for more education. Making generalizations is a poor way to interpret individual motives, but one does get impressions. The first decade's students were motivated to learn about America, then the most powerful nation in the world. By the 1970s Japan seemed to be the world's economic engine and the students wanted to help Americans learn about Japan. Most recently, they have wanted to improve themselves. Over the fifty years, by far the largest number simply wanted to broaden their experience.

"This is a chance that may
never come my way again."

"I will be able to look at my own country
from a different viewpoint."

"And in living in an environment with students from all
over the States and the world—all with different backgrounds—
I will get to know more about different ways of thinking,
how to get along with different kinds of people, and more about
human relationship."

"Of course I have no doubt that
St. Paul's will improve my English
at a much higher level too."

"They say that St. Paul's School stands
on a beautiful and broad campus."

"I hope to develop my spirit of independence
and learn to stand on my own legs."

"I have long dreamed of going to America,
because I thought that it would
be a good chance to broaden
my experience."

"Another reason is that I love sports. Being at St. Paul's
School, whose students are all sports-lovers, means for me
a wonderful chance to learn something of the 'true basketball.'"

CHAPTER 2

'We Wish to Continue'
The First Decade

Professor Mamoru Shimizu, Makihara's English teacher at Seikei, followed his distinguished student's progress in America. St. Paul's twice had advised Seikei of Makihara's exemplary record. He "...contributed a great deal to our school last year," Frank Lloyd wrote, "and we were all very fond of him...a remarkable boy...our debt to him is great." This pleased Shimizu and the Seikei teachers. They now believed that other Seikei students would also benefit from a year in America. Surely, since Makihara did so well, Seikei students could handle the work if their language skills were good enough.

Professor Shimizu wrote an exploratory letter to the SPS vice rector: "I understand from Makihara that you again desire to admit one or more students from Japan." He advised that he had a student to recommend "if such privilege were made available." Lloyd promptly responded positively: "St. Paul's School is indeed interested in enrolling qualified Japanese students. We would be only too glad to learn about the candidate to whom you refer in your letter. A recommendation from you naturally would carry great weight."

These first feelers led to a year-long exchange of letters to select a second Seikei student for admittance to St. Paul's. The Director of Admissions, Thomas W. Nazro, tried to describe the kind of candidate the school wanted: "If we are going to do our part in improving

Mamoru Shimizu, Seikei principal emeritus, English teacher, recruiter and forebear of SPS graduates, with granddaughter Karen.

the mutual understanding between the East and West, it seems to me that we must do it through superior students." Nazro explained gently that the student would have to meet SPS's entrance requirements and overall academic standards, giving allowance for the difficulty of testing and studying in a foreign language. Shimizu understood that "knowledge of English alone was not sufficient in such a case."

To help evaluate the candidates, SPS wanted the Japanese boys to take the Junior Scholastic Aptitude Test. The math portion of the test was to be taken as a measure of general intelligence; SPS understood that the English portion would be difficult. "We have regular entrance examinations for boys coming to this school, and if I were to send those to you, would you be willing to administer them...?" The test, Lloyd explained to Shimizu, "is an examination of aptitude and general intelligence."

Shimizu had mixed reactions to this news. He felt relieved that he would not have to make the difficult decision whether the boy could handle the academic work at SPS. But he feared "[the boy] will be dumb-founded in part, for the range of vocabulary is quite different. We must ask you to make ample allowance for the difference." Shimizu sought advice about the test from a friend, Frank Lang, an Englishman at the Foreign Language College in Tokyo. Lang was "rather taken aback" by the test, commenting to Shimizu that the questions were "awfully difficult" for Japanese boys. Nevertheless, SPS had requested it so the test would be given.

Having made clear that the boy must meet SPS's admission standards, Nazro raised another perspective: "We feel that a Japanese boy who comes to this school is a real representative of his country, and as such, must be an outstanding boy to justify our accepting him." St. Paul's was now suggesting that it would only consider an application from a student "measuring up to your highest standards." St. Paul's wanted to consider only the very best Seikei could offer.

The 1950–51 exchange of letters settled on some rather vague criteria. They were understood—if not perfectly, at least well enough. Seikei would select its best candidates and then St. Paul's would consider whether they met its standards for admission.

During this defining time, two candidates came under discussion. Ultimately, they did not run the still-forming gauntlet. One failed to meet SPS's academic standards, and the other's enthusiasm for study abroad waned. In spite of the apparent difficulty in selecting the perfect candidate, Seikei very much wanted to send another boy to St. Paul's. The Japanese apologized for the trouble the disappointing selections caused. But, Shimizu concluded, "our care and trouble have contributed a great deal to our mutual understanding, I firmly believe."

Seikei continued to look for outstanding boys eager to go to America. Shimizu confided: "Meanwhile, we are thinking of how to choose suitable students for the next scholastic year. We are going, if you have no objection, to collect several candidates by informal announcement, and then fix the best one or two after open discussion." St. Paul's School had no objection.

In April 1951 Lloyd received a letter from Ichiro Suzuki, principal of Seikei High School: "It gives me great pleasure to recommend to you Tatsuo Arima, who has just finished the first-year course of our school, as a candidate for a scholarship in your school." The letter enclosed transcripts confirming an "excellent" scholastic record in all academic subjects. A companion letter from Professor Shimizu to

Nazro, neatly fitting Nazro's selection criteria, recommended Arima as "one of the very best boys not only from the scholastic point of view, but also from his character." His teachers extolled Arima's character: "sincere, dutiful, and very humble, with a touch of child-like innocence...he has got an ability for mastering any intellectual subject." Before he was born, Arima's parents had lived several years in Oakland, California, where his father served as a Methodist minister. Arima sounded good to Lloyd and Nazro.

Considering his youth, Arima did well on the Junior Scholastic Aptitude Test. Seikei's enthusiasm for him signaled that he was one of their best. Younger than Makihara had been, Arima had three years to finish high school. The prospect of having a Japanese student for three years appealed to SPS. When the admissions committee read in Professor Shimizu's letter that Arima had trekked for over two hours in knee-deep snow to get to school one day, he was in—he could handle the New Hampshire winter. Arima was accepted to enter in the fall 1951 as a Fourth Former.

He received the news "beaming with expectant eyes." His English language skills needed improving so SPS recommended that he work on them before arriving in September. Seikei Principal Suzuki wrote to Frank Lloyd. "In behalf of our school, let me express our deep gratitude for your generously accepting him.... Particularly we are grateful to hear that you have taken special notice of our opinions, and we sincerely hope that Tatsuo will contribute to our mutual understanding.... We believe that Tatsuo will receive a great deal of advantage by a longer period of study with you...."

St. Paul's School again paid all the educational expenses for the Seikei student but he was expected to pay his travel expenses to get from Tokyo to Concord. The College Women's Club, a group of Japanese and American women who had attended American colleges, had been raising travel money for three or four Japanese students a year, and they paid for Arima's one-way ticket to America.

The 17-year-old scholar enthusiastically prepared. At the time, the United States required immigrating students to submit stool samples to the U.S. embassy doctors to test for tapeworms. Lung X-rays had to be taken, sealed, and carried to the port of entry. Young Arima did all this, procured his visa, and practiced his English.

In late August, friends, family and teachers waved farewell from the Yokohama dock. Arima boarded *Koei-Maru*, a freighter bound for

Friends and family surround Tatsuo Arima (holding hat, center) as he leaves Yokohama for America in 1951. Yoshiaki Shimizu stands at Arima's right; to Shimizu's right stands Arima's father.

Seattle. It is easy to imagine the emotions such a young man would have had—excited anticipation tempered by fear and loneliness. Home and everything he knew soon disappeared over the horizon. Arima's "touch of childlike innocence" would soon disappear, too.

Arima described what happened on his arrival in Seattle thirteen days later. Immigration officials stopped him. Arima had arrived a few days after ministers of the United States and Japan had signed the peace treaty that ended the military occupation of his country. The American occupation forces that had issued his travel documents no longer had authority. And, Arima wrote in the SPS *Horae Scholasticae*, an examining official said "my health certificate from Tokyo St. Luke's Hospital was not satisfactory…. 'X-ray and the test of red blood-corpuscles will be required'…. He spoke slowly and distinctly. But it does not mean that it sounded kindly or warm. I do not remember the rest of his talk, for I was not listening, or rather, I could not understand him after all.... In a few minutes I found myself in a cell with two blankets and a pillow. The sound of a key lingered in my ears for a while after a guard left. There were three young Chinese men.... Iron bars prevented us from reaching the windows or trying to escape.... I had to recognize that I could not expect any help.... I felt as if I had been swallowed.... Soon afterwards I found out that my roommates had infectious diseases.... I feared I would be infected. That night I could not sleep."

Arima was taken to a hospital for tests the next morning. "A young doctor told us that it would take six days to get my results.... I knew I would be driven crazy if I had to stay in that dreadful cell any longer.... I could do nothing except lie on the bed...." Intense humiliation gripped Tatsuo. "I did not want to go home. How could I see my friends and masters in Japan who had just sent me off?" Already he had failed.

The next afternoon a Methodist pastor, a friend of his father's whom Tatsuo did not know, secured his release from the bureaucracy, toured Seattle with him, and saw him onto the train east. For four days he rolled 3,000 miles alone. He was not happy. Even his Bible did not wholly comfort him.

The second: Tatsuo Arima who graduated a year early, 1953.

William A. Oates, the new director of admissions, met a lonely, frightened boy at the Concord terminal "with that genuine warmth of his." The Oates family took him into their home until school started. Tatsuo remembers the "overwhelming kindness" with which he was received. Those days with the Oates formed a path to friendship that endures 50 years later.

"I was accepted by the students of St. Paul's with all the sentiments you would expect from that generation of boys—generosity and tolerance towards a young boy who would not understand either their language or their cultural traits...for the masters and the parents of the students, experiences and memories of the war only six years earlier must have been a very vivid part of their emotional and mental makeup. Therefore the meticulous care with which they prepared my arrival, the overwhelming kindness they showed me, are astonishing. In spite of their recollection, or perhaps because of their own experiences during the war, they tried so hard to make it possible for a foreign student to adjust himself in this rather unique social milieu."

Arima entered St. Paul's life with intensity. He immersed himself in the school's athletics, excelling in gymnastics and wrestling. He was one of the fastest boys in school. Nick Platt '53 remembers a typical sight: "Tatsuo Arima [of the Fourth Delphian intramural football team] running hell for leather down the field with his helmet perched on the back of his head and a long trail of people all trying to catch him." In the spring he joined the track team as a sprinter. Friends shortened his name to "Tat."

Arima's English proved no obstacle to success. He had little difficulty reading and writing English, but, he says, "did so with the kind of meticulous slowness you would associate with a novice reading the Thomistic text in Latin." He studied hard, often after "lights-out" curfew, working in the bathroom sitting backward on the toilet using the "porcelain water container" as a bookstand. He improved his speaking and writing skills by participating in the Library Association, Concordian Literary (and debating) Society, and the Propylean Literary Society. The excellence of expression and vivid description in his story, "From the Immigration Office," quoted above, testifies to his beautiful command of English. Arima studied German, too, and joined the German Club, *Der Deutsche Verein*. "Leonard Barker was my favorite teacher; [Robeson Peters'] American history and sacred studies were the most meaningful courses."

Frank Lloyd reported to Professor Shimizu: "Tatsuo, as you gather, is doing an excellent job in every way. He is well liked by his classmates and by his teachers. He is one of the top-ranking students in his class, and he has taken part in all the athletic activities that we offer.... There is no question that Tatsuo has added a great deal to our life here, and we are indeed glad that he is a member of the school. Our special thanks go to you for having sent him to us."

In the spring of 1952 in his first year at SPS, Arima competed for the Ferguson Scholarship, the oldest and most prestigious academic honor St. Paul's School awarded. Established in 1882, it is awarded annually to those members of the Fourth and Fifth Forms who write the best examinations in four disciplines in a series especially set for this scholarship. Arima won the Fourth Form Ferguson Scholarship. The humble Japanese boy, whom Immigration had detained and whose teachers worried about his ability to study in English, had achieved one of his school's highest academic honors in his first year.

He completed the Fifth Form in exemplary fashion. Then "Tatsuo has decided to enter college in September 1953 rather than stay a third year at St. Paul's School," Oates reported to Professor Shimizu in November 1952. "Although he made such a fine record here, we shall be sorry to lose him but we can understand fully his desire to go on to college and we are in complete agreement on the wisdom of this step." Arima graduated *magna cum laude*, as a Fifth Former.

The summer after graduation Arima worked at the same Quaker camp near Woodstock, Vermont, at which Makihara had worked. He entered Harvard, graduated with honors in government, and went on to earn a doctorate. In 1961, with his formal education completed, he returned to Japan to begin a career in diplomatic service. He had been in America for ten years.

In the fall of 1952, Oates asked Professor Shimizu if he was "acquainted with another young Japanese boy of abilities similar to or approaching those of Tatsuo, who might be interested in coming to St. Paul's School beginning in September 1953.... We are ready again to grant full scholarship aid and whatever additional help is necessary to make it possible for a Japanese boy to come...."

Seikei was indeed acquainted with a student of ability. Principal Ichiro Suzuki conferred with Professor Shimizu, who had so successfully selected the previous two students. Professor Shimizu described the boy as "very very eager to go to your school... however, there is good reason for me to be as much scrupulous about this as

Arima and Shimizu, staffers at Timberlake Camp, 1954.

possible. To be frank, this boy is really 'unusual.'" A month later, Professor Shimizu had conquered his scruples. "It is Yoshiaki Shimizu, my second son."

Carefully avoiding any hint of bias, Professor Shimizu described his son at length in humble detail, including all the blemishes, childhood illnesses, and likes and dislikes in study. He then arranged letters of recommendations from teachers within and outside of Seikei School. He translated these testimonials into eloquent English, apologizing for his inadequacy: "The Japanese original was written in such soft, warmhearted tone, so characteristic of the writer's personality, that it is very difficult to reproduce it adequately in English."

Yoshiaki had organized the Seikei School Junior Red Cross. The assistant national director of the Junior Red Cross praised his humanitarian leadership: "This is worth mentioning about a young man of the country like Japan where the leadership in the meaning of citizenship and community service is most noticeably lacking, due to its historical and geographical isolation from the rest of the world for centuries.... After an adequate training and education in the country of humanism and democracy like America,...Yoshiaki will surely make an excellent future leader for the good relationship between the two countries on both sides of the Pacific Ocean."

The third: Yoshiaki Shimizu, cum laude *graduate, 1955.*

Young Shimizu had won a series of regional and national oratorical contests in English. "His English speech," his class master wrote, "is not like one of those made by aliens...it is one expressing his own thought in his own language, with feeling properly diffused...so natural that we forget that we are hearing a speech made in a foreign tongue...."

On a more lighthearted level, one teacher wrote, "He is always open-hearted, witty, with a fair share of youthful pleasantry (I mean jests and pranks)." Peering deeply into his son's emerging character,

'We Wish to Continue'

Yoshiaki's father recognized "an artistic bent, with a good sense of beauty."

St. Paul's School, impressed with the volume of material, administered the tests and readily accepted Professor Shimizu's second son, Yoshiaki. "I am delighted..." Oates' letter began. The Shimizu family was overwhelmed. "I wish I could describe to you how he ejaculated his joy on hearing the good news," Professor Shimizu wrote. "And how he was actually moved to tears when I showed him your letter. With trembling choked voice he expressed his thanks to me. We, father and mother, were deeply touched."

"I wanted to go to America," Shimizu has revealed. "I had a very peculiar experience with American kids whom I befriended around my neighborhood. I saw American kids argue with their parents. I had never seen anything like that.... I said, 'Boy, what a wonderful country to go to.' I had this romantic idea about America, even before St. Paul's. I was so happy—there was a sense of unreality. Gosh, yes, I would definitely go to America—this is happening!"

The Shimizus visited with Tatsuo Arima's parents and Mrs. Makihara, who was then planning a trip to America. They consulted Bishop Viall, who had made the original connections between SPS and Seikei. A picture book of St. Paul's impressed Yoshiaki. "Somebody told me St. Paul's was like an English public school. You have an image of American boys living like Mr. Chips' students. The Chapel...a studio picture of Mr. Abbe looking down...a puffy li'l kid...scenes of the dining room...they are doing some artwork and all wearing neckties. To picture myself among these kids—that was something."

The American consul's office in Tokyo processed Shimizu's visa smoothly, and the family battled the Tokyo municipal bureaucracies and the Bank of Japan for permits and money for the trip. Professor Shimizu gave his son a gift to deliver to Rector Henry Kittredge—a copy of *Dictionary of English Quotations with Examples of Their Use by Modern Authors* of which the professor was an editor. "Your donation will be prized highly in our library," wrote Kittredge. This book was the first gift from Seikei to St. Paul's School.

The Shimizus carefully planned their son's journey to St. Paul's. English teacher Lang had friends in San Francisco. From the U.S. Army's period of occupation, Yoshiaki knew some American boys now living in Albuquerque, New Mexico. His ship would arrive in the United States sooner than immigration authorities would prefer

Future Bishop Frank Griswold and future Professor Yoshiaki Shimizu study US popular culture in Drury Hall, 1953.

because school did not start until mid-September. Immigration evidently did not want him to become a ward of the state—how would he be supported until school started? The problem was solved by a planned visit in Albuquerque and SPS's promise to care for him. Comforted by the knowledge that on arriving in America friends would meet him, Shimizu boarded the Nissan Company freighter *Nikkei-Maru* at seven in the morning, July 26, 1953, bound for San Francisco.

He traveled with about a half-dozen college and graduate students, one attractive woman among them. He was the only high school student—by far the youngest. They all depended on the graces of the *Nikkei-Maru*'s chubby, gregarious captain, who threw parties every night so he could dance with the attractive woman.

For thirteen days Shimizu steamed across the Pacific to San Francisco, then he rode more days on a train to Albuquerque to stay with his friends for a few weeks, and then on through Chicago to Boston. "I was very lucky in that when I got on the train at North Station, Boston, I met this young teacher who kept looking at me. Then he asked me, 'Are you the new student from Japan?' When I heard this question I was so relieved that somebody knew about me. He was Bob Eddy. He was the first SPS teacher that I met."

Oates was waiting at the Concord station for Shimizu's train. He met and drove him to school. "As the car was coming along Pleasant Street going to the campus, this is exactly what the photograph shows! Then I saw the chapel to the right and I thought, 'Wow, that's real!' It's like suddenly everything you envision in the pictures is there."

Oates asked Shimizu to stay in their third-floor room; he lived with the Oates family for a week. He met the Lloyd boys, the Warren boys, and ate at Hargate dining hall. His dorm room in Drury needed a bookcase. "I built the first bookcase in my life," he said. Mr. Hill, carpenter and woodshop teacher, helped him out. "I had time to prepare."

Shimizu worked hard his first year, battling language difficulties and new subjects. "I spent many nights in that room sweating over homework, sometimes using a flashlight in bed to read page after page of difficult English assignments, since there was a rule that said we were to be in bed by ten or so." A classmate and dormitory neighbor, Frank Griswold, befriended him after noticing that Shimizu was terribly homesick and that other boys seemed not to pay him much attention. Now the Presiding Bishop of the Episcopal Church, Griswold recalls that being Shimizu's friend had special benefits: on the occasions when Shimizu received packages from home, they held a Japanese evening, sitting on the floor in robes or kimonos, eating Japanese delicacies.

Shimizu played Isthmian intramural club soccer and wrestled on the SPS team. He became known as "Yoshi." Following in Makihara's footsteps, he entered the Hugh Camp Cup public speaking competition and won. In America as in Japan, Shimizu was a prize-winning orator. The *Horae Scholasticae* awarded him the Williamson Medal for his poetic prose essay, "Chasing the Moon." "Admirable for its sensitive observation, skillful use of detail, and directness of statement," said a faculty reviewer. "So, after all, I was already a humanist!" the proud Shimizu says. As the two years closed, Shimizu moved up in class rank to become one of the school's top scholars. He graduated *cum laude*.

He had done well in the math tests, and Lloyd, director of studies in 1953, thought he might be headed for a career in science. But Shimizu found himself more and more often in art teacher William Abbe's studio learning to express himself in drawing and painting. Abbe took him to the Boston Museum of Fine Arts to see an important exhibit of 90 pieces of Japanese art sent by the Japanese government as a post-war gesture of friendship. Shimizu became president of the SPS Art Association and won the Anniversary Art Prize as well as the Ellsworth Greenley Prize for excellence in artistic work.

Professor Shimizu, humbled at his son's good fortune, thanked Abbe: "You have been, particularly during the first year of his life at your school, a great solace to him in his lonely hours, and even after he got used to his new life at school he could find a great deal of delight in your company. The adventures he could have in the field of art, which you kindly arranged for him, will prove, I have no doubt, unforgettable experiences in his later years."

After briefly wondering whether he should attend a smaller school with a good art program, Shimizu went to Harvard. He did take four years away from Harvard to attend art schools in Hamburg, Germany, and New York City. The "open-hearted, witty" scholar with "a good sense of beauty" received his bachelor of arts degree in art history from Harvard in 1963. Twelve years later, he received his doctorate from Princeton, and was ready for an academic career in art history and a life in the United States.

The budding relationship between St. Paul's and Seikei might have ended in 1955. At the end of the 1953–54 school year, Henry Kittredge retired. Without Kittredge's continued inspiration at SPS, the three Japanese students might have represented just a brief brilliant flurry of post-war altruism. A tremor rippled through the Seikei connection, too. Professor Shimizu no longer knew personally any suitable boys at Seikei. The Japanese may have worried that under a new rector SPS might not as generously accept and pay for more students.

The Reverend Matthew Warren became rector of St. Paul's School at the close of the academic year in June 1954. His election to St. Paul's followed years of activity in Christian education. He had served as the first director of the Education Center of the Diocese of Missouri, and rector of parishes in Macon and Atlanta, Georgia. He had spent three years preparing for the St. Paul's School job, visiting schools and alumni, but he was unknown to the Japanese.

Warren undoubtedly knew that St. Paul's needed to grow physically and culturally, as world and domestic trends began to affect it. Under his guidance, the first African-American faculty and students joined the school and plans were made to enroll young women. Athletics, arts, and classrooms were expanded and in a variety of ways St. Paul's reached out to the community and the world.

Matthew M. Warren, seventh rector of St. Paul's School.

Minoru Makihara, about to graduate from Harvard in spring 1954, prodded Professor Shimizu and the incoming rector to continue with Japanese students at St. Paul's. "Minoru has written Mr. Warren about organizing more formally the selection of students in the future who might come to St. Paul's and who might come from your school," wrote Lloyd, the director of studies. Professor Shimizu replied to Warren in September. "Minoru has often written to me about his enthusiastic idea of establishing on a more or less permanent footing an arrangement concerning scholarship students between St. Paul's School and his old school."

Before returning to Japan, Makihara visited Warren. He reported to Seikei his conversation with the new rector: "Speaking warmly of the students from Seikei, [Warren] said: 'Ben, we have been very pleased with the performance of you and the other Japanese boys we have had in the past years. In the future, we wish to continue to welcome students from Seikei on a school-to-school agreement basis. Will you convey our plan to Seikei when you get home?'"

Christianity for the Japanese

Buddhism and Shinto are the traditional religions of Japan, although Christian missionaries have worked there and made converts. By interesting circumstance, an Anglican Bishop in Tokyo started the Seikei connection and the first three Seikei students grew up in Christian families. Later Seikei students had varying reactions to the Christian presence at St. Paul's School.

"Honestly speaking, I felt very uncomfortable.
I had never been religious and, moreover,
in this aspect world where freedom of religion exists,
it was hard for me to take part in religious activities
which were almost compulsory."

"I was impressed by its art and ceremony,
and I enjoyed them."

"It didn't bother me."

"We are not used to going to church in Japan.
It was a new experience
and I was interested in it."

"It was foreign to me
and in spite of my honest attempt,
it was not for me.
At the same time,
Sacred Studies taught by John Walker
was one of the most influential courses."

"It felt strange to me to be singing the hymns
and saying the prayers that read 'Almighty God....'
Now organ music reminds me of St. Paul's."

Chapter 3

'Rich and Rewarding'

The Sixties And Seventies

Matthew Warren had no thought whatsoever of losing the Seikei source of outstanding foreign students. "I was quite interested in the suggestion of Ben Makihara and Tatsuo Arima that we undertake to formalize our relationship in Japan with a committee who would administer an operation similar to the Rhodes Scholarships," he wrote Professor Shimizu in October 1954.

Shimizu and Seikei's Principal clearly preferred the informality that had worked so well so far. Shimizu replied, "...if the selection is to be limited to the Seikei High School alone, there would be no necessity of setting up a committee.... Things would go more smoothly if I took on the office of recommending.... Personally speaking, the choice will be the same whether there is a committee or not.... Minoru seems to be too anxious to realize his idea, so I referred to this matter just to respond to his enthusiasm." However, Seikei reluctantly expressed willingness to do whatever SPS desired in the way of formality.

Having not thought out the details of such a formal procedure and undoubtedly busy with his new duties, Dr. Warren deferred the idea of a committee. "I think we will hold everything concerning a possible committee to work with you until after you have received back to yourselves the boys you have so generously sent to us, and perhaps in the years ahead between all of us we can be sure we have some perpetual relationship."

Yoshiaki Shimizu would graduate the following spring. Warren quickly moved to quench any fears in Japan that the relationship might not continue. In October 1954 he wrote to Professor Shimizu. "We are again in a position to consider the application of another Japanese boy for entrance here in September 1955. This letter is to urge you to keep us in mind and feel free to send on an application, if you feel you can do so. It is a most gratifying thing to have this warm relationship with you...."

Professor Shimizu was delighted to hear this. He had been hoping for a suitable candidate. The Seikei faculty had a boy in mind that Professor Shimizu did not know personally, but by December he had enough information and the confidence to recommend Toshimichi Hirai to St. Paul's.

Hirai was a top student, president of the Student's Association, and possessed "a calm and gentle disposition." He had "remarkable leadership...some hidden power of commanding the love and respect of others." Oates sent the Junior Scholastic Aptitude Test, a practice exam, and requests for transcripts and recommendations. Hirai completed all to the SPS admissions committee's satisfaction.

The Hirai family received the news of Toshimichi's acceptance "bursting with hilarity." They promptly set about the difficult job of obtaining the U.S. visa and arranging transportation. Then, Hirai was off to America. Like Makihara, he sailed from Yokohama on a freighter bound for New York via the Panama Canal—another two-month odyssey. His stay at SPS began traumatically. He broke his jaw in soccer practice immediately after his arrival and a translation mistake caused terrible consternation in Japan until word arrived that he had survived! After a seven-week recovery, Hirai excelled as a student, graduating *magna cum laude* and going on to Harvard. The Seikei "warm relationship" had survived the change of administration at St. Paul's.

At about this time, Professor Shimizu stepped away from his exclusive responsibility for selecting applicants. The next year, 1957, Motoi Samuel Okubo entered St. Paul's for a successful two-year preparation for Harvard. Okubo was the first student to have been admitted without the informal tutelage of Professor Shimizu, who must have participated in Okubo's selection but in a more consensual way. (Shimizu soon left Seikei to take a position at the new International Christian University.) A Seikei faculty committee had selected the SPS scholarship student, beginning what was to be a continuing practice. Thus, Warren had not needed to push for "formalizing our relationship with a committee."

As a step toward setting up a more routine selection and admissions process for the Seikei students, SPS developed an application form to be completed by a boy's parents. It has been used since 1957 with relatively little change. Aptitude testing and the requirements for transcripts and recommendations remained. The school required no different information from the Japanese than from any other student. The math part of the aptitude tests was evaluated for general intelligence, and the English part was greatly discounted to allow for the language difference. Otherwise, SPS had utmost faith in the Seikei applicants because the previous selections by Professor Shimizu and the faculty had been so outstanding.

The Seikei scholars kept coming, one every two years. In the early 1960s jet air travel became commercially possible. Hachiro Nakamura '61 described his journey to New Hampshire in 1959. "All the flights from Tokyo had to refuel in Hawaii in order to reach the West Coast, and, of course, air travel was reserved only for the extremely wealthy, business people, government officials and so on…. I must have been frightened to death about the journey…but, then I was a fearless youth, and courageously threw colorful tapes and confetti from the deck of a freighter to my family and friends who came to see me off with banners and flowers and to say '*Sayonara.*' I was off to sea and never returned…[my] 11,000-ton ship sailed under the Golden Gate Bridge after 13 days…. Then came the relatively new non-stop transcontinental flight…. I arrived in New York in the middle of the night."

During the 1960s many students in the United States revolted against tradition and authority. "There appears to be no end to the restlessness," Matthew Warren wrote, "and our own community is not, nor should it be, unaffected." As the decade ended, SPS was on its way to co-education, and its religious orientation had been significantly tempered. The narrow, traditional curriculum had expanded to over 100 courses, including an Independent Studies Program (ISP) in which students could fashion their own study projects.

Eleven Seikei scholars attended St. Paul's through the quiet 1950s and the tumultuous 1960s. Yoshiharu Akabane, Junji Shioda, Kaoruhiko Suzuki, Eijiro Yamauchi, and Kiyoshi Yoshiko Kikyo followed Nakamura. Although travel conditions had eased somewhat with the advent of jet air travel, these scholars faced challenges similar to those of the original Seikei students. Their country was still recovering from war, the SPS curriculum and teaching methods were strange, and they could not get home easily. In addition, coming from a land of traditionally Buddhist and Shinto beliefs, some were unfamiliar with Christian ritual, still a significant part of SPS life. Some had not lived outside Japan or had not spoken English outside a classroom. For them, studying in a foreign land must have been excruciatingly difficult. In spite of the struggles, seven of these outstanding young men graduated *cum laude* or *magna cum laude*. Nine of the eleven went on to Harvard.

In appreciation of their American education and to honor the 20th anniversary of the first Seikei student's arrival, the first eleven Seikei-SPS graduates presented to SPS a beautiful stone *yukimidooroo*, literally a "snow viewing lantern," actually a lantern to light a snow covered path. This expression of appreciation by the growing number of Seikei-SPS alumni now stands inscribed with their names on the shore of the pond near Hargate Hall, where it remains a quiet reminder of the two schools' relationship.

All the Seikei students during those first 20 years, except the very first, stayed at SPS for two years each. Seikei had sent a new student every other year. When one graduated, a new student entered the following fall. All went on to American colleges. This pattern settled into routine throughout Warren's term as rector.

Seikei administrators probably found the alternate year selection quite comfortable. They could be selective, and if students one year did not show enough interest in traveling away from home, there would be the next year. As the decade of the 1970s arrived, Japan was recovering economically and prospects within the country had certainly improved. The Japanese had learned much from "all over the world." Now that Japan was more prosperous, interest in learning in America—the "wonderful country"—tended to appeal to young people looking more for a foreign experience than for further education. Although bright and adventurous, these students might not necessarily be Seikei's most distinguished academic scholars.

The changes in Japan, an increase in Asian-American student

enrollment, and another change of command at SPS presented possibilities for drought in the flow of Japanese students to St. Paul's School.

In 1970 William A. Oates became rector of St. Paul's. The 55-year-old Harvard graduate and native of South Dakota had served his school for over 20 years, as teacher, registrar, director of admissions, and vice rector. For many of those years he had greeted the arriving Seikei students in Concord, and driven them the last few miles to school. As rector, he has written, he would continue to help

William A. Oates, eighth rector of St. Paul's School.

"push a sturdy, parochial institution, securely rooted in 19th–century traditions, into modern, national perspectives."

When Oates succeeded Warren as rector of St. Paul's, the Seikei faculty must have been comforted because they had known Oates well as director of admissions for many years. They knew him to be a strong supporter of the relationship between the two schools.

But the new rector did have a change for them. Admission to the most prestigious American colleges was getting more and more competitive. For 20 years Harvard had received all but two Seikei students from St. Paul's. In the future that high level of acceptance simply was not going to continue, regardless of the students' abilities. Oates did not want Seikei to assume any longer that St. Paul's was an automatic stepping stone to Harvard or any other top American university.

At one time Seikei administrators may well have believed SPS and Harvard were somehow connected. In 1960, Satoru Nakajima, a Seikei English teacher, had thought of SPS as a "dream school": "All the Seikei students went to Harvard after St. Paul's, and this fact led me mistakenly to think that St. Paul's was affiliated with Harvard, situated almost next door to it." The Japanese had almost sensed accurately. At this early time in the Seikei relationship, Harvard's dean of freshmen and an admissions committee member was an SPS alumnus and former SPS faculty member. St. Paul's relations with Harvard were cordial, but each student always had to prove qualified for admission.

In 1971 Oates wrote to Seikei about his concerns. He very much wanted to continue to have Japanese students of high quality at St. Paul's. He and others must have considered very hard what the college admissions squeeze might mean for the Japanese. How would they react to learning that an SPS education might not ensure a good college for their boys? Would they drop the affiliation with St. Paul's?

Something had to be adjusted to remove any unrealistic expectations. Sanford R. Sistare, director of admissions at that time, suggested that the Seikei scholar come to St. Paul's for one year rather than two. The student should plan to return to Japan at the end of the year. This way, SPS could still provide an annual scholarship without feeling responsible for the Japanese student's admission to an American college. Planning a short stay and return, no Seikei student would expect admission to an American university.

Oates and Sistare worried needlessly. The Seikei administrators were eager to continue having the opportunity and privilege of study in America for their top students. Besides, now the trip from Tokyo to Boston took just hours by air, not weeks by boat. The fare had become affordable. The prospect of a long-term absence need no longer inhibit interested students. It was much easier, quicker, and cheaper to get back home. A student need not lose opportunities in Japan. A single year abroad would entice students in a way that the prospect of a six-year absence could not. Seikei readily agreed to St. Paul's new suggestion.

In 1971 St. Paul's School had become co-educational and could offer Seikei women the opportunity to study in the New Hampshire woods, too. The first Seikei scholar under the one-year plan was a sporty young woman, Kaoru Iida. She entered SPS in 1972 as a Fourth Former with a one-year scholarship commitment. Three years later she graduated and returned to Japan for college at the International Christian University in Tokyo. Her successor in 1975, Amy Yoshiko Nobu, also stayed three years, as did two more of the seven Seikei students who entered in the 1970s. The "one year and return" plan never happened. All stayed at least two years. All but one returned to Japan for college.

Like their predecessors, they found study in a foreign land difficult. "I was frantic," recalls one student. "I struggled. Like most of the other Seikei students, I did not understand most of what everybody was saying." "I was just scared to open any door," said another as he searched for his way around the dark dorm on his first night. All students lived in the dormitories, but vacated them for vacations. "It was always very stressful to have to figure out whether I had a place to stay during vacations," said one student, explaining a typical and recurrent problem. "Some of my friends were kind enough to invite me to their homes, and visiting them was a very good experience."

Well-intentioned parents had offered naïve advice: "There was absolutely nothing to worry about life in America provided that I chew food quietly." In fact, the Japanese students encountered many surprises. "Till towards the Thanksgiving, I sat on the toilet facing the wall," one remembered. "I hope you appreciate how astonished I was one evening to see the foot of a student in the next alcove pointing to the opposite direction from mine." A fire drill confused Kaoru Iida: "I immediately went out with my shoes and coat on, following the way I was taught in Japan. What I saw there were many students barefooted without coats.... I ran back to my room and took them off and I became the last person. The dorm master told me, 'You are not only late but also barefooted!'"

Classwork was hard, too. "How am I to study in English and communicate...?" worried Hachiro Nakamura. "Imagine that I was trying to read The New York Times editorials, memorizing Shakespearean sonnets, and also studying German at the same time...." But they persevered, found help, learned, and made friends. Yoko Nishikawa recalls, "I think it took me a few hours to translate one page of my assignment for the English class. So my friends, who thought I would never finish my homework on time, decided to perform the content of the reading assignment like a play. I would never forget their kindness." Some students found solace and friends in sports and music. For Hana Sugimoto, "Piano did not require any language skills, so it was relaxing and relieving, especially when I was frustrated."

After a sacred studies class, Akari Yamaguchi revealed to a classmate that she felt "like a caged bird" because she "was unable either to drop the course of religion or to understand [Paul] Tillich. Then [my friend] said that she had also been feeling like a caged bird. After that, every day, we talked about 'why it is impossible to understand Tillich' jokingly. And when we began to realize that Tillich's opinions made some sense and we both found the exit of the cage. After several months our friendship was cemented and unbreakable."

The 1970s marked the first period in which more than one Seikei scholar attended St. Paul's at the same time. Without interruption, beginning in 1975 and lasting to the present, a Seikei student has entered SPS each year, usually in the Fourth or Fifth Form. In 1979 and again in 1989, two Seikei students entered. During this period only two have spent just one year. All the others stayed two, three, or four years. But none entered Harvard. All except four returned to Japan for college in the 1970s and 1980s, but in the 1990s nine Seikei students matriculated at American colleges, including Georgetown, Columbia, Tufts, Wellesley, and Johns Hopkins.

SPS continued to grant a full scholarship for the first year of study. When the stay was extended, St. Paul's continued the scholarship without any appraisal of need. The money came from general scholarship funds. Two Seikei students enrolled as tuition-paying students. Ever since Oates restructured the program in the early 1970s this general plan has been maintained.

St. Paul's School's Japanese alumni recognized the tremendous impact their SPS experience had made on their lives. As Japan recovered from the war and began to compete with the United States as the world's foremost economic power, they understood better than most the profound importance of maintaining understanding between the two countries. They felt a spiritual responsibility to do all they could to maintain the flow of students between the two countries.

The Japanese alumni kept in touch with each other while at college and later, meeting occasionally to relive their experiences, as alumni everywhere do. As soon as there were enough of them, they informally created a Seikei-St. Paul's Alumni Association. Led by Minoru Makihara, the SPS alumni, graduates of American and Japanese colleges, sought ways to support the scholarship program.

Yoshiaki Shimizu, who lived in the United States, spoke for all the Japanese alumni in a 1974 letter to Oates: "Our experiences have taught us that the satisfactions that we obtain from our effort to understand the people of this country [USA] and be understood by them transcend by far anything that formal diplomatic relations between the two countries can establish. Although our contributions are statistically unmeasurable, we feel that our life both in the U.S. and Japan and our personal contacts with the people of this country, either through our calling or through social life is bridging the two countries in the way that the politics or economics cannot achieve." Then Shimizu added the promise that all implicitly made: "I shall pledge my financial support as well as spiritual help for the program, which finds no parallel in this country."

Sometime in the mid-1970s, the Japanese SPS alumni joined the Seikei faculty in selecting students to apply to SPS. Commenting on the committee selection process during his term as rector, Oates noted, "The one unchangeable characteristic of this program has been the very high quality, intellectually and personally, of each of those chosen. How wonderful it is that, now, the selection committee for new scholars is composed of alumni of Seikei and of St. Paul's School, providing knowledge of both institutions and both school experiences, which helps insure careful, thoughtful consideration."

The foreign students at St. Paul's formed the International Society in the 1978–79 school year. Students of all nationalities and ethnic groups (including Americans) were invited to share cultural experiences. The interest and energy of its members determined the extent and quality of the Society's activities, which could vary greatly from year to year. Sponsored events frequently included an "International Week" with a bazaar and entertainment. When inspired, the Society prepared foreign foods, sponsored international films, and conducted art, dance, music and other cultural experiences for the entire school. The Japanese frequently stimulated the Society's best activity.

The Conroy Visitors Program had begun under Matthew Warren in the 1950s. Under this program, SPS invited noteworthy visitors to address the school. Over the years outstanding poets, politicians, adventurers, artists, scholars and other leaders visited the school for several days of meetings and talks with students and faculty. In the 1970s the Conroy fellowships included Harvard Professor of East Asian Studies John King Fairbanks in 1973, and one of America's leading authorities on Japan, former Ambassador to Japan Edwin O. Reischauer, then a professor at Harvard, in 1976. Seikei scholars Yoshiaki Shimizu, then a curator of Asian art at the Freer Gallery of the Smithsonian Institution, and Tatsuo Arima, a Japanese diplomat, also lent a distinctly Asian air to the Conroy program during the decade.

This activity was stimulated, at least in part, by Japan's economic recovery. By the mid-1970s Americans noticed more and more Japanese automobiles on California highways. The small cars used little gas, needed little service, and were comfortable and easy to handle. Sony's brilliant color television pictures outshone those on Zenith, RCA, and Motorola sets. Commentators and academics began asking why Japan's business methods were so successful. "Made in Japan" was no longer pejorative. All over America, Japan was receiving attention in the New Hampshire woods, too.

Friends: Leon Ochiai and Timothy Ferriss, 1994.

The presence of more Japanese students on campus at SPS highlighted a growing interest in Japanese language, history, and culture in the SPS community. The Seikei students noticed that Americans held many misconceptions about Japan. For example, at a time when Sony television sets were inundating the United States, Amy Nobu '78 was asked, "Is there TV in Japan?" She was so concerned about this apparent ignorance that one morning she spoke from the chapel pulpit. "We Japanese are very interested in your country. Why do no American students ever go to Japan?"

Nobu argued that Americans needed to learn the Japanese language and travel to Japan if they were truly to understand the Japanese culture. Seikei and St. Paul's should have a true "exchange" of students, she urged, not the one-way program that existed.

Shortly after hearing Amy Nobu ask why no Americans had vis-

Friends: Amy Remus and Yoko Nichikawa at St. Paul's, 1990.

Friends: Michiyuki Nagasawa and Prescott H. Logan, 1991.

ited Seikei, Sixth Former Stephen G. Vaskov proposed as an Independent Study Program (ISP) project that he go to Seikei to observe a foreign school and participate in various campus activities to broaden his horizons. He attended Seikei for two months in the spring of 1976. Two years later, Loring McAlpin '78, following Vaskov's example, won the Heckscher Prize for submitting the best ISP proposal. He also proposed to experience Seikei. McAlpin attended Seikei from January to March 1978. Neither Vaskov nor McAlpin knew a word of Japanese when they left St. Paul's. But they had started something.

At the decade's close, to mark 30 years of continuous Seikei-St. Paul's friendship, the Seikei-St. Paul's Alumni Association sent a magnificent collection of books about Japan and Seikei prepared a small commemorative booklet. Seikei gave St. Paul's a mounted calligraphy scroll by artist Shinzan Kamijo, one of Japan's most distinguished calligraphers. The scroll hangs at the top of the stairs at St. Paul's Ohrstrom Library, displaying the verse, "Peaches and plums utter no words, yet underneath a path will form," the Seikei school motto.

Rector Oates honored the occasion by inviting the Seikei Junior and Senior High School principal, Masahiko Okuzumi to visit St. Paul's during a "Japanese Week" from February 4 through 8, 1979. Yoshiaki Shimizu, then an associate professor of art history at the University of California, Berkeley, and Stephen Vaskov, then a student at the University of Pennsylvania, also attended. Sheldon Library displayed the magnificent books in its rotunda. Seminars and films on Japanese culture were presented. Shimizu lectured on "Two Traditions within the Japanese Culture" and spoke to art classes. Vaskov encouraged students to consider the opportunity to study in Japan.

Principal Okuzumi attended classes and student organization and faculty meetings. "On one occasion," wrote Terrence M. Walsh, advisor to the SPS International Society, "arriving at a tea given in his honor by the International Society, Mr. Okuzumi bore gifts of multiple Origami games, rice paper balloons, and cartons of rice and seaweed foods! In full swing, the party was quite a scene." Talking with the American students, Mr. Okuzumi even revealed that the Japanese had problems with student activism in the 1960s, too. His son had been student body president at Seikei in 1968. "He led our school's only demonstration to get back our auditorium, which had been closed down by demonstrating college students. They got it back!"

Okuzumi spoke at a morning chapel service about the Seikei-St. Paul's relationship and was warmly received. "I have long wished to visit St. Paul's School," he said, "to thank everyone concerned for their great kindness over the 30 years. I am deeply grateful to Dr. Oates for inviting me to join you in celebrating our schools' relationship and for giving me the opportunity to realize this long-cherished wish."

On the last day of Okuzumi's visit, the student council passed a charter revision that read in part, "From this day on, the President of the Seikei High School Student Council, upon election, will become an honorary member of the St. Paul's School Student Council...we wish this to begin a sisterhood between the two student councils."

Okuzumi was deeply moved by the friendship he felt in Concord. "Mr. Okuzumi was in tears when we all had our parting heart-to-heart talk at the Barretts on the last eve of Mr. Okuzumi's stay," reported Shimizu, who also was moved by the memories of "wintry years" in Japan, and the "extraordinary" history of Seikei and St. Paul's.

At the decade's end, Oates expressed on behalf of St. Paul's School the Americans' sentiments: "For 30 years we have welcomed and been enriched by students from Seikei. The steadfast friendship over these years of each of these students has been remarkable. We have enjoyed correspondence, we have cherished visits by our—and Seikei's—alumni, we count on their continuing interest in us, as we have interest in them. We want in the coming years to continue and increase this rich and rewarding association."

Events in Asia in the 1970s had puzzled Americans. Witness, the United States could not control the quagmire in Vietnam and Japan had returned to the world scene. Some said that Japan had failed to conquer the Pacific with its army and navy but that it would conquer with its economy. By 1980, Japan's extraordinary recovery had made it America's economic rival.

For over a century St. Paul's School, along with most American schools and colleges, had focused its curriculum on Western civilization. Language studies centered on Latin and French, with a few students taking Spanish or German. But during Oates' tenure as rector, SPS had responded to the growing interest in Japan with the first hints of an effort to learn and teach about Japan. Two of its students had traveled briefly to Seikei and visiting scholars had lectured about Japanese culture and relations. The Seikei students, faculty, and alumni had helped and stimulated SPS. They gave books to its library, talked to its students, and Seikei continued to send scholars. But no American students had yet studied at Seikei.

The growing economic competition between the United States and Japan could shatter—or prove—the Seikei-St. Paul's premise that person-to-person friendship at an early age will increase understanding between nations.

SPS Rector William A. Oates and his wife, Jean, visit a class at Seikei in 1982. Teacher Takahiro Hiraoka explains the lesson.

CHAPTER 4

'Even More Interesting'

The Eighties

When the 1980s arrived, foreign students from many nations and Americans from many ethnic backgrounds attended St. Paul's. As one Seikei scholar described it later, "The diversity was stunning. There were students of all races from all over the U.S. The campus seemed so colorful with their fashion, language, mannerism, and attitude, being so heterogeneous."

St. Paul's had no organized method for helping foreign students with English. When they saw a need, some teachers did arrange extra tutoring sessions with the Japanese, but there was no formal English as a second language (ESL) instruction. English faculty member Alan Hall recalled, "Looking back on that time, I realize how indifferent we all were to their problems: We just let them take what everyone else was taking and made a modest allowance for the dictionaries they were always using." The Japanese and others struggled, asked Americans for help, and learned quickly. But with more and more foreign students now attending, the need was obvious, and in 1987 St. Paul's hired an ESL teacher.

Kathleen Zimpfer has offered tutorial sessions to SPS's foreign students in both academic and communicative language areas for thirteen years. At Elmira College she had majored in international and Japanese studies and had been an exchange student in Japan for ten months, taking extensive language training at Nanzan University and living with a local family. Before coming to St. Paul's she had taught ESL at the University of New Hampshire while she studied for her master's degree in English/linguistics specializing in ESL. Her sessions with the SPS students included study of language patterns, adapted media materials, and cultural projects, in addition to needed language tutoring.

In 30 years, 18 Seikei students had attended St. Paul's. A Japanese student from Seikei now arrived each year. But only two American students had visited Seikei in those three decades, and for only two months each. Rector Oates and Principal Okuzumi discussed this imbalance during the celebration of Japanese Week in February 1979. The two leaders wanted to make the exchange truly two-way and they agreed to seek ways to encourage American students to spend a year at Seikei.

Certainly the language barrier was a major obstacle. All Japanese students learned at least some English early in school. But virtually no Americans learned Japanese in elementary or high schools. The SPS students who had visited Seikei, Vaskov and McAlpin, had gone without knowing Japanese at all. Although they got along for the short time they were there, their experiences were necessarily limited. Some previous Japanese language instruction was essential if SPS students were to attend Seikei.

Few, if any, American secondary schools offered Japanese language courses. The language was deemed too difficult for high school students, and schools could not support a course for the small number of students that could be expected to enroll. A few colleges and specialized language institutes offered intensive Japanese courses; high schools simply did not teach the language. That SPS would offer a Japanese language course was a startling prospect.

The SPS Independent Studies Program offered a vehicle for students to create their own learning experiences. The first SPS students to visit Seikei had traveled abroad pursuing personal independent study projects. Could this program become the vehicle to learn—or to teach—Japanese?

It took a Seikei student to push the idea. Amy Nobu had thrown down a gauntlet in the chapel. Two years after she graduated, one of her Seikei successors picked it up. Kaori Kitazawa, an industrious and sensitive young woman, had entered St. Paul's in 1978 as a Fourth

Former. That first year, she decided on her independent study project for the next year: She proposed to teach Japanese.

She planned and prepared a beginner's course, working at SPS and, during the summer, in Japan. Her advisor in this project was Terrence M. Walsh, a counselor with experience and study in youth psychology. Toshiko Phipps of the School of International Training in Brattleboro, Vermont, also helped Kitazawa design the course. The intensive work necessary to plan and teach the course led Walsh and Kitazawa to spend considerable time together. After her graduation, they would marry.

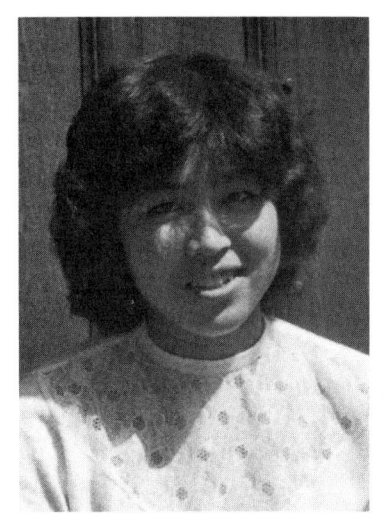

Kaori Kitazawa, student and SPS's first teacher of Japanese.

In September 1979 Kitazawa offered St. Paul's first class in Japanese language. "When we received an announcement in the mail of the new Japanese language program, which was to be started as Kaori Kitazawa's senior project," Tara McGowan '84 remembers, "my father encouraged me to take up Japanese, saying that if I liked Western calligraphy, Japanese brush calligraphy would be even more interesting. Knowing little more than this about Japan, I enrolled in classes." Six Americans—five students and a teacher, the head of the SPS Modern Languages Department André Hurtgen—signed up for Kitazawa's class.

That year eight Japanese students were at SPS, including Seikei scholars Yoichi Hiraki '81 and Haruki Minaki '81. Each of them volunteered to tutor and work with one of the Americans. "There was an immediate sense of camaraderie among the students that first year, blended with the excitement that comes from being part of an experiment," McGowan recalls.

"Kaori's project entailed learning the language as an infant would, without the aid of written language, but we all chafed a bit at the limitations this imposed, especially me, the writing system being one of the things that had attracted me to the language in the first

'Even More Interesting'

place," says McGowan. "The class was unusual, not only because it began as a psychology experiment, but also because it was part of a larger experiment to launch an exchange for the first time from St. Paul's to Seikei, and I think we all felt some responsibility for the success of this new venture. A network of interested and dedicated parties formed around the class. We were all assigned tutors from among the Japanese students on campus. I remember mine was Sono Aibe, who was unrelated to Seikei but who turned out to be a conscientious tutor and friend nonetheless."

St. Paul's first Japanese language class lasted the full year. Kitazawa proved a superb teacher, Terrence Walsh an effective advisor. "The network of friends and people interested in the program made it a central focus of my first two years at St. Paul's, both inside and outside the classroom," says McGowan. For her efforts Kitazawa won the St. Paul's Honor Scholarship for exceptional scholarship. Her work, perhaps more than anything else, stimulated St. Paul's to greater awareness of the value of teaching Japanese culture and language.

The response to Kitazawa's course so impressed Oates and Hurtgen that the faculty decided to start a formal Asian Studies program. Walsh was given the job of recruiting someone to build the program and he turned to Seikei-SPS alumni.

Walsh contacted the third Seikei-SPS scholar, Yoshiaki Shimizu, now in Washington, D.C., after finishing several years of teaching at Berkeley. Among his students had been Richard Okada, a young Japanese-American doctoral candidate from California. Shimizu suggested him to Walsh.

Walsh called Okada, who was then in Japan, and told him about St. Paul's and about the opening. On a visit to Japan in 1981, André Hurtgen interviewed him at a video game table in a bar. Okada was well qualified, if not over-qualified for the job, having studied Japanese language at Stanford and the Inter-University Center for Japanese Language Study in Tokyo. He had earned a master's degree in Japanese literature at Berkeley, was pursuing a doctorate in Japanese literature, and had taught three levels of Japanese for four years. A grant for dissertation research had taken him to Japan, where he met with Hurtgen.

Okada arrived at SPS in the fall of 1981. He taught second-level Japanese to those who had taken Kitazawa's class, and first-level to beginners. Ten students enrolled. He introduced them to the written *hiragana* and *katakana* phonetic syllabaries (characters representing sounds) and they learned a few *kanji,* the Chinese characters representing ideas and objects. Trying new ways to teach language, he incorporated video, audio, role-playing, memorization, and dialogue with "lots of drilling." Seikei and other Japanese students helped unofficially and the class formed a Japan Club, did calligraphy, and took field trips to Boston museums. "All," Okada remembers, "were very receptive, very enthusiastic, very excited."

By 1983, although enrollment was still small, there were enough interested students that Okada introduced a third-level course. Tutoring independent study projects related to Asian language or culture was added to his assignment. Okada had given the Japanese language program a firm foundation. But he was a higher-level academician; deep research studies stimulated him more than teenagers struggling with a difficult language. He believed others could better build and improve the program, so at the conclusion of the 1983–84 academic year, after three years at SPS, Okada returned to Berkeley to finish his dissertation.

For much of his 30-year career at St. Paul's, William Oates had met the Japanese students in Concord and corresponded frequently with Seikei. As director of admissions, then vice rector and rector, he had nurtured the Seikei friendship.

In 1982, three Americans had studied at Seikei, and two were in the midst of their studies there. SPS had educated twenty Seikei students, and SPS was teaching Japanese language classes. Seikei's Principal Okuzumi had come to St. Paul's two years previously. But in 30 years no SPS rector had visited Seikei. Okuzumi had invited Oates to Seikei, but while rector he did not want to leave his responsibilities at SPS. In retirement, Oates was ready. "I knew that no rector had visited, and I thought therefore I should go. I left the school in June 1982, and made the trip to Tokyo the following October.

"From the moment of our arrival at Narita Airport...Mrs. Oates and I were treated with overwhelming thoughtfulness, with careful and efficient concern for every minute of the day...following plans that had been carefully drawn up." Under the "wonderfully friendly and thoughtful" guidance of Satoru Nakajima, Seikei's coordinator of exchange programs, the Oateses saw the sights of Tokyo, a *kabuki* theater performance, and met Kikuzo Tanioka, executive director of the Seikei Alumni Association, before going to a restaurant 40 stories above Tokyo for a private dinner given by Tatsuo Arima and his wife.

The next day, at Seikei they met the principal, Choji Yokote, who received them over tea. Then at an outdoor assembly of the school, standing on a small boxlike podium before 1,500 Japanese and with Nakajima translating his words of gratitude and pleasure, the first St. Paul's leader to visit Seikei presented to the school an SPS chair, a bowl, and a Chapel Service book. "For some of you, the possibility now exists, at your leisure, of sitting in the St. Paul's chair while reading from our Chapel Service book, at the same time sipping Coca-Cola from the St. Paul's bowl!"

Oates and his wife toured the campus, met other high-ranking officials of the school and university, and then returned to their hotel for the evening's reunion banquet. In the hotel's banquet hall, teachers, alumni, friends, and parents gathered for drinks and exotic delicacies.

"For celebrations, such as this evening," Oates recalls, "there is a Japanese custom of breaking open a keg of *sake* with mallets. Not on the first stroke. Three strokes must be taken. So as the ceremonial part of the evening was about to begin, Jean and I were given mallets and asked to break open the keg with three strokes! To everyone's relief, we succeeded."

The keg opened, *sake* toasts followed—toasts to the institutions, to people, to friendships. Then Oates was introduced. Speaking extemporaneously, he put the celebration in perspective: "We bring greetings from all of St. Paul's School...this means from about 9,500 people....

Rector and Mrs. Oates prepare to hammer open the keg of sake.

64   A GENEROUS IDEA

The period we celebrate is a long one: 30 years, and now 33 or 34. Can it be? Yes, it is, half of my lifetime! What a long time, truly it is." The former rector recounted his memories of Japanese students at SPS: "Through so many wonderful students, now strong adults, we feel very close to your school and your country. In this very important way we know you well, even though this is our first visit here.

"We cherish this significant educational and human enterprise, an activity of the highest quality which has advanced the spirit of cooperation between our countries. Long may our two institutions flourish. And may the spirit of friendship between Seikei Upper Secondary School and St. Paul's School live forever."

Oates then distributed gifts to everyone present. The former and current principals each received Chapel Service books. SPS black, red, and white ties, a set of blazer buttons, and a book went to Nakajima, Tanioka, and each of the senior alumni. SPS plates went to alumni parents, who treasured scenes of the school they had never seen. Hundreds of items were distributed. "The presents were sensationally received," Oates reported.

Speeches by Tatsuo Arima, Minoru Makihara, and Kiyoshi Matsumi '70 followed and the celebration closed with clapping and smiles. Everyone left for home, but Oates could not yet rest. Makihara had planned a business meeting after the banquet. Although it was late, it was the only time he, Arima, Nakajima, Tanioka, and Oates could get together to discuss seriously the exchange program's objectives, student selection, admissions, and colleges. It

Oates, the first SPS Rector to visit Japan, and his wife celebrate with Seikei friends Tanioka, Arima and Nakajima (with Mrs. Arima).

'Even More Interesting'

was time to stop sugarcoating the relationship and get down to work.

Speaking as concerned friends, the three alumni representatives wanted to make sure things continued to improve. These men had always supported the relationship fully and enthusiastically, but they were concerned that the Japanese students from SPS were having difficulty getting into colleges in America and Japan. Why? Were their school records not good enough?

There had been a dramatic change. The first nine had gone without exception to Harvard. Indeed, only three of the nine Seikei students since 1971 had attended American colleges: Pomona, Trinity, and Princeton. The other six students returned to Japan to attend six different Japanese universities.

But after celebrating exhilarating successes, the Japanese had concerns about continuing that success. Were SPS and Seikei missing opportunities for their graduates at the best Japanese and American colleges? Harvard, revered in Japan, had not admitted an SPS-Seikei student since Kaoruhiko Suzuki in 1967. Had the quality of students selected for scholarship decreased? Could the selection process be improved?

Ten years earlier Oates had tried to explain to Seikei the extremely competitive college entrance atmosphere in America. Not only was college competitive, Oates explained, but it was also harder to enter St. Paul's. Nearly every applicant was capable; nearly everyone admitted chose to attend. "I sketched the present level of competitiveness for American students who apply for St. Paul's School, and the extreme difficulties experienced by the admissions committee in the past few years in making final selections of a finite number of candidates to be admitted in the face of large numbers of highly qualified applicants. The Seikei people were surprised to hear this, and apparently had no idea of the degree of competition that now exists."

In the discussion that followed, Oates learned that Seikei had felt obliged to nominate a candidate to SPS each year in order to keep the scholarship active. If the nominees were not up to SPS standards, Seikei thought that SPS would not accept them. Seikei learned that the SPS admissions committee assumed that all nominees had the full confidence of Seikei and hesitated to turn down a nominee, always accepting one each year.

This was pretty consistent with the understandings that had existed at the beginning when Thomas Nazro defined what SPS was looking for, but circumstances had changed greatly since then. SPS had no shortage of applicants. In Japan, greater opportunities attracted the top students. Academic leaders were not necessarily interested in study abroad. The teamwork between the Seikei selection committee and the SPS admissions committee had drifted into "an 'After me, Gaston' situation," as Oates termed it later. "Neither group want[ed] to offend the other, nor to make a judgment that would seem to cast a doubt, to say nothing of an aspersion, on the other group."

For two hours the group worked. The former rector, no doubt wearied by jet lag and *sake*, the Seikei alumni representatives, and Seikei's coordinator of exchange programs found understandings for the future. None of them could control the outcomes, but they could bring to their respective institutions very persuasive recommendations. And they did so.

Makihara, Arima, Tanioka, and Nakajima understood better the admission situations at SPS and in American colleges. They would do their best to recruit competitive students and would feel no obligation to make a nomination they were not able to approve fully. SPS, for its part, would understand if no nominee surfaced, and could feel free to reject any nominee. Everyone remained fully committed to the program. The Seikei men reiterated pride, gratitude, and appreciation.

The rest of the Oateses' stay was a whirlwind of sightseeing in historic Kyoto and Nara, experiencing traditional food and hotels. Their "warm and thoughtful" host saw them, exhausted and exhilarated, to the Narita Airport.

André Hurtgen, Belgian-born teacher of French and Spanish at St. Paul's since 1960, headed the Modern Languages Department for twenty years. While a young teacher in the late 1960s, Hurtgen had been master at Ford House. A Seikei student, Kaoruhiko Suzuki '67, had been a supervisor of younger boys at Ford. Hurtgen was impressed with this exchange student. "The more I got to know him, the more I wanted to find out about this mysterious place, 'Say-Kay,' and this exotic land peopled with supermen." In the ensuing years, he read avidly from Japanese books the Seikei alumni and the Nobu family had given to SPS. He even joined his students in Kaori Kitazawa's beginning Japanese language class. "Within the first hour I was bitten—and that changed my life!" Hurtgen says.

Hurtgen had become enamored of Japan and things Japanese. He continued his study of the language and in 1981 he and his family traveled to Japan. Hurtgen was also harboring an irresistible yearning. He made a visit to Seikei, and met some of its leaders to explore the possibility that he might teach at Seikei. This trip "strengthened my desire to live and work with Japanese people in their own ambience."

The following summer, Hurtgen had an unusual request. "I am due for my sabbatical leave," he advised the rector. "I want to go to Japan to teach at Seikei School." St. Paul's new rector, Charles H. Clark, had spent twenty years in the Far East in Episcopal Church missions, and he understood Hurtgen's desire.

André Hurtgen, SPS modern languages teacher for thirty-five years.

While at Seikei in October, Oates had discussed Hurtgen's proposal and received Seikei's confirmation that a position would be offered him to teach conversational English. Thus assured, St. Paul's approved Hurtgen's sabbatical proposal, including, with the "very generous cooperation of department colleagues," the unusual midterm departure in April to accommodate the Japanese school schedule.

Hurtgen arrived at Seikei in April 1983. He joined the *Eigoka Kenkyushitsu* (English Department offices) where he prepared classes, graded papers, shared meals, held "hundreds of pleasant conversations, thousands of cups of tea," and made lasting friends.

Hurtgen taught conversational English at junior high, senior high, and college levels. He found his students frustratingly unlike Americans—he faced a classroom thoroughly trained to avoid offense and to conform to the norms of peer acceptance. "I was struck time and time again by the change that takes place when the *sensei* (teacher) enters a classroom full of boisterous and energetic youngsters. With the ceremonial '*Kiritsu*!' (Rise!), '*Rei*!' (Bow!), the room becomes silent, heads are bowed, faces become blank and expressionless. As the teaching starts, joy leaves the room. The *sensei* lectures, and the students write it all down. No queries, opinions, dissents, or discussion. On the rare occasion when the teacher does ask a question, all heads bow even lower as the students seek to evade the teacher's gaze. I found it a Herculean task to get a conversation started in my 'English conversation' classes. Such a simple question as 'What day is today?' would be met with stony silence...my Japanese students were acting exactly as their society expected. By addressing a point-blank question to an individual...it was I who had acted in an improper and unsettling fashion.... How could I possibly teach English to boys and girls who would not answer the question 'How are you?' without first consulting their peers?"

Hurtgen did find ways. "Often, after an almost fruitless 'English conversation' class, one or two of my charges would approach me politely and beg: 'Please, Mr. Hurtgen, I want to speak English.' And then, over a cup of coffee, away from the threatening ambience of the classroom, we did succeed in communicating."

The overwhelming conformity in the Japanese school struck him. Uniforms erased economic differences, imparted a sense of belonging, supported discipline, and disguised and retarded students'

While in Japan, Hurtgen practices shodo, *the demanding art of classical calligraphy.*

'Even More Interesting'

maturity. Individuality could be expressed only in slight variations in skirt length, or scarf knots. One Sunday, he met a "little girl from his class" who had offered to take him to a museum. At the train station, he looked for the quiet, prim child he had seen only in a neat blue uniform. Instead he saw "an attractive young lady in high heels, wearing costume jewelry, and just a touch of makeup.... 'Mr. Hurtgen, I *am* seventeen, you know!'" she said to the astonished American *sensei*.

Hurtgen was privileged to attend a meeting of the Seikei committee to select the candidate for St. Paul's. "When the committee met to interview the twelve applicants, I was invited to be an observer—it was made clear to me that I was not to ask questions or express an opinion. I was a *gaijin* (foreigner) and therefore not part of the system. The head of the seven-member committee would ask a question (e.g., Why do you want to go to America?) to student #1 (who, of course, had no time to prepare an answer, except for the fact that he must have known that it would come), then repeat the exact same question to student #2, student #3, and so on. Of course, by the time student #12 was questioned he had had ample time to prepare his answer. And so on in similar fashion to question #2, #3, etc. Such a procedure perfectly reflected the Japanese love of orderliness, precision, and fairness. After all, each student was asked the same question, right? At the end of the meeting, the committee met behind closed doors and selected the 'top' three candidates...."

Tara McGowan recalled the second step in the process. "[T]here were two girls and one boy. One girl was shy and did not say very much. She seemed very young to me. The other one expressed herself eloquently and without any inhibition and seemed self-possessed and mature for her age—all qualities American schools look for in a candidate. I was convinced that any St. Paul's admissions officer would immediately single her out, so I was astounded to learn, at the end of the session, that the younger one who had barely uttered a syllable above a whisper was the one they chose.... It made me wonder at the time about a selection process where the value systems are so at odds."

McGowan explained, "When I had some time to reflect on it, however, I realized that in Japan the younger girl would be considered more appealing because, as they pointed out at the time, she was *sunao*. This is often translated as "naïve" but it really connotes more a kind of simple openness of heart or mind or even a kind of vulnerability. There is no doubt that in Japan girls are expected to be *sunao*, but it is not entirely derogatory since nearly all people there strive to be *sunao*, and, if you are not, you are in danger of having difficulties relating to other people. But *sunao* is not something Americans consciously look for or value. We want people in schools or in job interviews to seem like they know what they are doing even when, inside, they probably do not. We expect sophistication and even a so-called 'healthy cynicism' toward the world. I think this is one of the fundamental differences between the two countries...."

A select committee of Seikei faculty and some alumni representatives, often including Makihara, participated in selecting students. Whether or not Seikei or SPS really made any significant changes in the candidate selection process after the October 1982 meeting among Oates, Arima, Makihara, Tanioka, and Nakajima, the understandings they had reached seemed to clear the air. Changes in emphasis, recruiting energy, and mutual cooperation did result. Every year but one since then, a Seikei student has attended SPS on the scholarship and over 50 percent of the Seikei students graduating since 1982 have attended American colleges including Princeton, Georgetown, Johns Hopkins, and Wellesley.

While Hurtgen taught at Seikei, "He was the principal resource person as regards English usage for us Japanese members of the English department," Nakajima remembers. He helped and impressed Seikei teachers, who remain today appreciative of his work, hoping for another SPS teacher to come someday.

Because the Chinese characters used in the Japanese language could be pronounced in more than one way, Hurtgen had a "devilish" time understanding. He jokingly called it the "devil's language," and worked hard at learning it. He once asked Nakajima the Japanese word to use when someone sneezes. "Bless you" is intended to prevent the Devil from entering when the soul leaves the body in a sneeze, Nakajima had read somewhere. "We are not a Christian nation and do not believe in the Devil, and nobody generally says anything like 'Bless you' or even 'Gesundheit,'" he explained to Hurtgen, "But my wife does say something. When I sneeze loud, she says, '*Urusai-wane*,' which means "Don't make such a noise' or 'shut up,' *wane* being a feminine ending." Hurtgen heeded the lesson. As Nakajima tells it, a few minutes later, Nakajima sneezed loudly.

"There was a moment's pause, and then came a loud call, '*Urusai*!' That call was from Mr. Hurtgen."

He observed and absorbed Japanese culture and customs. Although occasionally unable to resist buying a juicy steak, he could eat anything, even "*fugu*, a kind of blowfish which is known for its potent toxicity as well as its good taste and good price, and which only licensed cooks could handle." He improved his Japanese vocabulary and grew comfortable speaking the language. He wrote about his experiences later, emphasizing contrasts between Japanese and American educational methods.

"What differences there are between our two schools!" Hurtgen wrote. "I mean, Kichijoji and Millville [the schools' precise locations] scarcely belong to the same universe! A campus one thirty-fifth the size of St. Paul's with twenty times as many students (most of them looking exactly alike in their uniforms)! The obedient and courteous demeanor of the Seikei students enchanted me, while their seeming inability to speak up in class drove me to paroxysms of frustration.... Teaching methods at Seikei and St. Paul's are poles apart, yet both schools do a first-rate job preparing their students for further study and for life. The very divergences in pedagogical approaches reflect the enormous differences between our two cultures...." By the time he left Seikei after one year he even felt confident that he could teach a beginner's class in Japanese language and culture.

Upon his return to St. Paul's in the spring of 1984, Hurtgen was greeted with the news that Richard Okada would depart to continue his graduate studies. Hurtgen promptly started a search for another Japanese language teacher. Fortunately, he soon found on his desk an application from Masatoshi Shimano, a student from Japan who was finishing his master's degree program at the University of Arizona. Shimano had excellent recommendations, a degree in education, and good experience. He had worked as a teaching assistant and had tutored elementary and high school students in Japanese. His inquiry also said he would like to organize extracurricular activities related to Japan. One attached recommendation read, "I believe the methodologies he is learning to be particularly well suited to high school age students...the reaction of the students has been positive." Who could be better for SPS?

Shimano had been looking for a teaching position and had sent inquiries to a number of private schools. The lack of response had been frustrating: A noteworthy 1983 report, *A Nation at Risk*, which severely criticized American schools, had not encouraged him. But his desire was strong.

Hurtgen replied to Shimano right away. The young Japanese teacher was immediately interested. As he said, "St. Paul's was one of the very few schools which had a Japanese program and the only one which had an opening."

Shimano, then 27, was hired and began teaching the Japanese language course in 1984. "My first few years at St. Paul's were enormously challenging (professionally very satisfying, but personally a very frustrating time), and a huge learning experience for me." He learned to handle the long winters and has continuously taught at St. Paul's for fifteen years.

Under Shimano's tutelage, the Japanese language courses have gradually improved and expanded, including up to five and sometimes six levels. Shimano enlivens his classes with Japanese cartoons, television programs, and songs. "At all levels," he says, "materials rich in cultural implications are used." Now, the SPS Language Center, with audiovisual facilities for 28 students, can show Shimano's skilled origami paper-folding demonstration simultaneously to an entire earphoned class, each member following his lesson on individual screens. The equipment allows students to do word-processing using the *hiragana, katakana,* and *kanji* written characters. By the time they reach the third-level course, students are reading and writing essays, discussing them in Japanese, and gaining fluency in everyday conversation. "Every school year…has been an equally challenging and inspiring one," Shimano says, "which makes me realize how much more learning, re-learning, and unlearning there are to be done…. The main object throughout is to attain basic communication competence."

A principal problem Shimano faced was attracting teenagers to the Japanese language. "Most of the students arrive with several years of French and Spanish behind them. They are understandably reluctant to abandon all that to embark on the study of a language which has the reputation of being difficult," Shimano says. Yet, in spite of the difficulty, enrollment has increased dramatically.

Starting with a handful, in two years Shimano had nineteen students. In two more years, 29 students were enrolled in his classes. In 1989, just one year later, Shimano happily announced, "Enrollment in Japanese has steadily increased and now, I think, with 41 students, it's the largest number ever...."

Kaori Kitazawa would have been astounded at the success of the program she had started with her small class in 1979, but she was not to see it. Kitazawa had married her advisor Walsh shortly after her graduation in 1981 and they moved to Japan, where he lectured and she continued her studies. One day in 1982, not long after they started their new life together, Walsh unexpectedly collapsed on the street and died. The young widow was unbearably distraught. To the shock and sadness of those who knew her, Kaori Kitazawa took her own life.

By the end of the decade, the SPS Japanese studies program, including the Seikei exchange, was attracting attention from other educators. Beginning in the early 1970s, St. Paul's had become the favored choice among students who also had been accepted at competing schools. Good relations with other New England schools produced candid conversations about their respective programs. "What are you doing?" asked administrators envious of SPS's recruiting success. William Oates says, "However much it may have been a determining factor in a student's choice—and it certainly was for some—the Japanese Studies Program was very much part of 'what we were doing.'"

Oates, Hurtgen, and others fielded questions from teachers and administrators. Hurtgen recalls spending several hours with representatives from Noble & Greenough School in Massachusetts, describing the history and evolution of SPS's Japanese exchange. Noble & Greenough later started its own Japanese course.

"The answers we gave about the Seikei program," Oates remembers, "involved finding a sponsoring school, an intelligent and committed faculty person at the other end, assigning full scholarship in one's financial aid budget to the student, assuring some funds for books and travel, locating an American 'adoption' family for vacations, assuring travel funds from Japan and return, finding summer jobs. In each case we described our activities."

SPS had created the first Japanese language study program among the major New England preparatory schools. By 1985, Russian and Chinese were being taught at St. Paul's as well. Rector Clark wrote, "Thus we are opening windows on a wider sphere of study than secondary education in America has heretofore acknowledged or embraced."

Rector William A. Oates addresses the assembled students and faculty of Tokyo's Seikei School during his visit in 1982.

During the 1980s, a Japanese school called Toin in Yokohama approached SPS and four or five other New England schools about setting up a summer program for American students. Toin wanted to establish connections with top preparatory schools. "They offered an essentially free-tuition six-week program," Hurtgen recalls. "Students live with Japanese families in Yokohama, [and take] classes taught especially for the Americans." Worried that this new offer might interfere with the Seikei exchange, Hurtgen promptly talked with Seikei about it. With its usual polite deference, Seikei replied that it would not be offended if SPS were to participate in the Toin venture. Subsequently, a number of SPS students and others have spent summers in Yokohama over the years.

Now with the Seikei-St. Paul's exchange truly a two-way program, its 35th year drew government praise in both nations. At a banquet at SPS in the fall of 1984, Rector Charles Clark received a letter of appreciation from Shintaro Abe, the Japanese foreign minister: "I take pleasure in expressing my profound appreciation to this eminent American school for the efforts and contributions it has rendered over the years for the strengthening of friendly relations between our two countries."

In the summer of 1985, Reverend Clark marked the occasion by visiting Seikei. At a reception with the Seikei-St. Paul's alumni he presented to Choji Yokote, Seikei's principal, a framed letter from the United States secretary of state, George P. Schultz. Schultz's letter reiterated the wisdom of Henry Kittredge and David Pyle. "The students…have formed personal and institutional bonds that have benefited mutual cooperation between our two countries," he wrote. "It is on these old friendships formed over generations, that the long-term success of our relationship depends." The 35th anniversary of the St. Paul's-Seikei program, he wrote, "was a significant event in the relationship between Japan and the United States."

Gifts were exchanged in these commemorations and during formal and informal faculty visits. For example, while on a bicycle trip through Japan, SPS art teacher William Abbe gave Seikei a pictorial map that he had drawn of St. Paul's School. Abbe had taught Yoshiaki Shimizu and scores of other students art appreciation and technique. His delightful map depicted the pastoral campus with cartoonish humor—whimsical beaver, deer, fish, birds, and turtles mingled in the trees and ponds among the chapel, Memorial Hall, Upper School, library, and dormitories labeled with banners.

It had been 40 years since Minoru Makihara stepped off the train in Concord after a two-month journey. During those 40 years he had progressed up the corporate ladder at Mitsubishi Corporation and had become president of Mitsubishi International, the U.S. arm of one of Japan's largest *keiretsu*s. All of that time he had led the Seikei-SPS alumni, helped recruit students, suggested improvements to the program, and lent his influence to its reputation. But, except for a few hours spent with rectors Warren and Oates, he had not been back to Concord. On November 2, 1989, "Ben" Makihara returned to his American alma mater.

SPS hosted a banquet in the athletic center, decorated for the occasion with calligraphy and banners. Several SPS-Seikei graduates and the current Seikei scholar attended, along with the program's friends Haven Pell '64 and Robert A. G. Monks '50. Nakajima and Hurtgen represented the faculties of their schools. Reverend Clark presided, spoke about the program, and read a letter from Seikei principal Mitsuo Matsuda.

The next morning Makihara addressed the school from the chapel pulpit, telling his respectful audience, "I am privileged to have this opportunity." Then Makihara reminisced about his year at school, summarized the exchange program, noting that it now included American students in Japan, and recalled teachers, administrators, and alumni who had made it happen. Then he spoke of the future:

"I believe we are going through a period of adjustment which causes stresses and strains on both sides resulting in a communication gap, which can only be overcome by the sharing of basic values and mutual understanding, based on personal exchanges like ours which are becoming more and more essential than in the past.

"Out of this special relationship between the two schools has emerged and is emerging a core of people who have a strong understanding of the two cultures and who will be essential in preserving and enlarging the bilateral relationship."

Dressed in school uniforms, students chat outside the chou-kan *or main building of Seikei High School.*

CHAPTER 5

"On the Heels of a Typhoon"

The Americans In Japan

Perhaps the first St. Paul's student ever to visit Seikei was Makihara's friend, H. Douglas Barklay '51. He spent the summer of 1950 staying in Tokyo with his father's friend, an Army officer on General MacArthur's staff. One day he met Makihara's mother and together they visited Seikei where Barklay spent a pleasant few hours talking and drinking tea on a lawn with Bishop Kenneth Viall, some of Makihara's friends, and several adults. No SPS student visited again for 26 years.

In the early spring of 1976, the Seikei teacher and exchange coordinator Satoru Nakajima was surprised to see SPS graduate Kaoru Iida '75 at his Tokyo home, accompanied by an American boy. "This was Steve Vaskov, the first St. Paul's student I had ever met with," Nakajima recalls. Vaskov wanted to join Seikei for a brief period to pursue his Independent Study Program project. He had not told Seikei of his plan, but the surprised school quickly accepted him. Nakajima recalls: "Until then only Seikei students had gone to join St. Paul's, and this imbalance in the relationship between our two schools had been more and more strongly felt among us. Anything feasible for us that would contribute to remedying the situation would have been welcome, which Steve's plan surely was."

Vaskov joined Nakajima's English class and several others as a

SPS-Seikei students Tanya Wilcox and Caroline Kenney, and friend Sharon Tohey, clown with Satoru Nakajima, who served as exchange student coordinator for many years.

guest student, and he practiced basketball with the team. Since he knew no Japanese, Nakajima said, "We thought that it would be worth his while to assist some of our teachers in English classes instead of sitting through all those classes in which he could hardly understand anything.... He responded to our suggestion with enthusiasm, and assisted us in various ways, as by teaching pronunciation, doing the model reading and conducting question-and-answer drills.... He acted as a sort of teaching intern, following the plans I had prepared for him."

Vaskov had arranged to stay with the Iida family, relieving Seikei of the need to find housing and a family able to take responsibility for him. "I was the first student ever to go from St. Paul's to Seikei. I had no knowledge of Japanese; I had to create with the teachers a program for teaching English; and I needed to make arrangements to live with a family in Tokyo. Despite these problems, my only regret now is that I didn't think of going to Seikei in the fall, for if I had, I would have stayed the entire year.

"For the first time I found myself totally immersed in the culture of a foreign country. Despite my ignorance of the language, living in Japan gave me the chance to learn about people in general and to begin to understand the culture of a country of great importance to the United States.... It was the people, though, that had the greatest effect on me. The regard and respect that the Japanese show towards others is one of the most outstanding features of the culture. The strict rules of formality have a tainted image in America, but this is because Americans see them in a different light. Where Americans see them as restricting the freedoms of the individual, the Japanese view them as a means of showing others the respect they deserve as humans. The nature of the language, people with colds wearing masks to prevent the spreading of germs, small storekeepers not worrying that people would steal, and the way that I was treated as a guest showed me some of the ways that the Japanese regard the importance of the lives of others."

The following year, Fifth Former Loring R. McAlpin wrote Seikei, asking what Vaskov had done. McAlpin was preparing an ISP project modeled on Vaskov's experience. Director of the ISP John Buxton supported the project and elicited Seikei's response: "We look forward to repeating the same delightful experience with Loring as a most welcome guest...."

McAlpin arrived in Japan on New Year's Day 1978 and was met by Nakajima and Kiyoshi Matsumi '71. Seikei had arranged accommodations with the Matsumi and Nakamura families, both parents of SPS graduates. McAlpin rested from his long flight on a *tatami* mat in the Matsumi's

Loring McAlpin clad for kendo, *in 1978.*

home, and then pitched into the school program Seikei had planned for him—a few days of regular classes, tutoring in Japanese with an Australian student, and assisting in some English classes as a "native informant." He joined the *kendo* team to learn Japanese fencing with

'On the Heels of a Typhoon'

Seikei Gakuen middle school and high school buildings, once surrounded by woods and fields, now stand in a suburban setting.

bamboo sticks. "We found him an earnest student and good mixer" during his two months at Seikei.

It would be three years before another SPS student ventured to Seikei. The two SPS visitors to Seikei each had made much of their brief experiences, but to study for a year required a longer, deeper commitment. Once the Japanese program had become established in Concord in 1981, American students quickly began to feel confident enough to attend Seikei for an entire academic year. SPS had now made it possible to fulfill the promise of Kitazawa's experimental introduction of the Japanese language.

Rector Oates had written Seikei to introduce Joseph Maybank IV who had graduated from St. Paul's in 1980 and who wanted to spend a portion of the following year in Tokyo before entering Harvard in the fall of 1981. Maybank prepared for his visit by studying the language and meeting with Professor Reischauer, the Harvard professor and former ambassador to Japan.

From January to June 1981, Maybank joined Seikei for a program arranged for him similar to that McAlpin had followed. "I took Joe to [beginning seventh grade English] classes to assist me primarily with pronunciation practice," Nakajima remembers. "He walked between the desks, and as he passed, made the individual students pronounce the words being studied.... Among them, however, was one boy who had spent a number of years in England. Each time his turn came, the boy would respond with his marked English accent. Joe seemed quite amused at this response, and would in turn respond, half laughingly, with a good-humored 'good,' although the boy didn't seem to copy his model at all."

Maybank's first impression of Seikei students as "wind-up toys that stood in neat rows and bowed at the slightest provocation" soon gave way. "Once they stopped bowing…my new schoolmates immediately reminded me of boys and girls that I had gone to school with for years in the United States." He had a Seikei uniform made, and tried to immerse himself in the culture as completely as possible for six months. The longed-for two-way exchange was ready to begin.

The first to go for a year were Elisabeth Bentel and Charles McKee. They had worked hard studying Japanese at SPS and Harvard summer school so they could spend their junior year at Seikei in 1981–82. McKee saw a chance to see the world and to witness the Japanese economic miracle first-hand. Bentel wanted to learn Japanese and, she joked, "get out of Latin!"

Seikei initially had qualms about accepting two students at once, but agreed when Oates emphasized how hard the two had been working for the opportunity. The schools agreed that the "basic principle" of one student each year thereafter would be observed. Nakajima was pleased to be able to personally tell André Hurtgen, then on his first visit to Tokyo, that the two had been accepted.

Flying from the East Coast through Anchorage to Tokyo, "Elisabeth Bentel and I arrived on the heels of a typhoon and I remember vividly the hot, moist air, pungent with the smells of late summer," McKee would recall. "The following day (Sunday) I rode out to school and was struck by the spacious handsomeness of Seikei's campus and the crowded jumble of neighboring houses."

Satoru Nakajima, "the person to whom Charlie and I owe everything," extended Bentel and McKee every possible kindness. As their "coordinator, advisor and tutor," he wrote their college recommendations, drove them to PSAT exams in his Volkswagen, and comforted them when discouraged. He was a tireless teacher, patiently explaining Japanese customs and culture as teacher, mentor and friend. His home and his time were always theirs for the asking.

Seikei arranged a special schedule so that they could receive tutoring in Japanese language, history, and culture. "The level of their Japanese was not such as to enable them to easily understand much of what was given in the regular classes," Nakajima says. "They also helped their Japanese schoolmates in their English study, Elisabeth assisting the English Club members when they put on an English play for the School Festival, and Charlie having a group formed…to whom he taught conversational English…." Indeed, they helped Nakajima, too, who was fascinated with English language usage and American colloquialisms like "driving range" [for golf], "borrow the telephone," and "walk-in." Principal Okuzumi reported to Oates, "Their speeches in Japanese impressed all. The targets of their studies here must be set at a very high level!"

The two Americans struggled with twelve courses. They took math, science, Japanese history, and even English. "After a summer school course at Harvard and previous year's study at SPS, I was ill-prepared for total immersion," confessed McKee. Individual or small-group language and calligraphy instruction helped them. "English was a laugh (I think I got the equivalent of a 'B'). Calligraphy was trying but fulfilling. Ancient Japanese ("*kanbun*") and science were totally beyond my limited capabilities."

They participated in sports and extracurricular activities as fully as they wished. "I loved *kendo* (except the cold morning practices) and *judo*," McKee remembers. Both he and Bentel reached *shodan*, the first *kendo* skill level, so that, like McAlpin, they each took home their bamboo sword, armor, and *shodan* certificates.

Bentel wrote a series of articles for the SPS student newspaper,

Elisabeth Bentel joins friends at the Seikei sports festival, 1982.

Icon of the SPS paper, Pelican.

the *Pelican*, describing, among other things, the Japanese group ethic, the New Year's celebration, communal baths, and travel conditions. McKee passed on to the *Pelican* some subtleties in using common expressions like *ohayoo gozaimasu* (good morning).

Both were very aware that they were pioneers. The Seikei Club held a dinner in Tokyo soon after they arrived, during which seven Japanese SPS alumni greeted them with welcoming speeches. "Through the speeches of the alumni and the founders of the organization, I began to see the importance of my year abroad," wrote Bentel for the *Pelican*. "I read many books about the culture of Japan before I came.... I pass days with an open mind, and find I learn more

Charles McKee horses around with Seikei friends, 1982.

about the people in a day than a whole book could ever describe. St. Paul's and Seikei provide that opportunity to learn about a country—not to learn about a stereotypical view." As an example, she wrote that Americans think that "Japanese are stern people who never smile, don't talk, and work all the time." Not so, she wrote; "Japanese people, however, are some of the happiest and [most] talkative people I have ever met; always friendly, never holding grudges, and extremely polite."

Seikei was pleased to have its two first American students. The school had urged SPS to make the student exchange a two-way pas-

On his first day at Seikei in 1981, McKee endures a baptism of fire: addressing his class—in Japanese.

sage. That had now come about. Thirty years before, Japanese students wanted to learn about powerful America. In the early 1980s, Japan's economy was the world's powerhouse and American students wanted to learn about Japan.

With the two-way exchange, the number of friendships between young citizens of the two nations had doubled. A tremendous step had been taken in accomplishing the goal both SPS and Seikei educators had set from the beginning. As Nakajima put it, "Personal friendships made on these exchanges are important in the world, because friends between Seikei and St. Paul's make best friends of Japan and America."

Twenty-one American SPS students have followed Bentel and McKee. A new SPS office—director of international programs—was set up to administer applications. The students had to arrange for their own passports and visas and meet the governmental immigration regulations. Japanese students endured similar procedures entering the United States.

These SPS scholars attended a school with 9,000 students; the senior high school section alone enrolled 1,500. The Americans were "visitor students" who studied a program designed especially for them. The Seikei School Alumni Association, representing all Seikei alumni, supported the cost of all exchange students to Seikei, including the SPS students, so the first year they did not pay tuition. In this way, Seikei reciprocated St. Paul's generosity with scholarships. Seikei also furnished all textbooks without charge.

Nakajima described an SPS student, who must have had a typical experience coping in class with the difficult language, in this way: "Although she had studied Japanese while at St. Paul's and had acquired the basics of the language skills, this was far from sufficient to enable her to follow the lessons given in Japanese. This is always the case with exchange students at their beginning stages here, and she must have found most of the lessons utterly unintelligible at first. But she sat through classes patiently, trying to understand whatever she could. In some subjects, however, the situation was better. In English classes, she could use the lesson hours not as those to learn English but to learn Japanese since there were plenty of translation and grammar exercises included. She also helped her teachers by performing model reading and assisting with Japanese-English translations at their request."

Tara McGowan '84 had several levels of language instruction before she attended Seikei. "All the letters I have received from her were written in Japanese," Nakajima marvels, "including the two which reached me even before her arrival for her year at Seikei…. She was thus bent on mastering Japanese with its complicated writing system, and when the time for the SAT tests came, she said she was sorry she had to take them in Latin instead of Japanese…"

For those less fluent in Japanese, getting along must have been grueling. Even McGowan tired: "I remember one morning finding it impossible to face going to school and needing desperately to hear English spoken, so I knocked on the door of the neighborhood Mormon missionary and begged to be allowed in, even though I had never met them. The wife was immediately sympathetic and laid out a futon for me to rest, and I spent most of that day just sleeping from exhaustion."

All foreign students wore the Seikei school uniform—for boys, regulation dark blue pants and jacket with high collar similar to the Japanese Imperial Navy officer's uniform; for girls, a white blouse with school scarf and dark blue skirt. Girls could not wear makeup

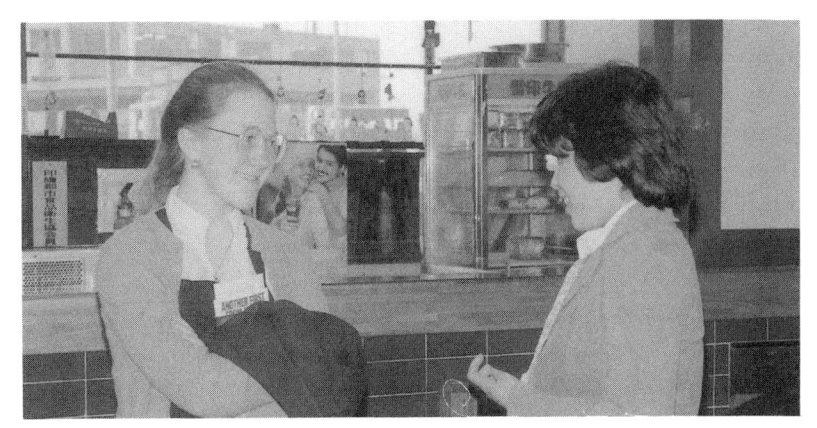

Kaori Kitazawa greets Tara McGowan at the Tokyo airport, 1982.

or jewelry. SPS had long had a dress code requiring jackets and ties in class and dark blue suits on Sundays, but by the time girls enrolled and its students went to Seikei, the SPS dress code had almost completely disappeared. Americans had trouble with the Seikei dress code.

"Although I was measured specifically for a uniform by a tailor, she did not quite seem to believe her measurements," recalls Joshua Brooks '86. "And so the trousers came back six inches too short and the waist was six inches too wide. I therefore spent the entire year slightly out of uniform." McGowan described her troubles. "Students were finding amusement at the sight of my socks that perpetually found their way down around my ankles…it was much later that I was initiated into the wonders of *sokutatchi* [sock-touch]—a glue that the girls actually applied to their legs to keep their socks from falling down."

Seikei, a day school, has no dormitory facilities but its administrators felt that visiting high school students needed adult supervision. Seikei had to rely on the goodwill of people to provide homes for its foreign exchange students. Host families took in the young Americans and other foreign students. The homes were small and often crowded. Hosting extra people meant considerable sacrifice, always made with exemplary kindness. McKee wrote, "The experience of living with the Shiozawas and Nakagawas, my host families, provided a window into Japan that has never been opened again."

'On the Heels of a Typhoon'

Nakajima explained, "Our policy has been to recruit such host families from among the parents of the Seikei students, trusting that, for the family themselves too, having an exchange student in their home constitutes a rewarding experience.... It is to a great degree due to their understanding cooperation that our valued exchange programs at high school have been able to grow and thrive over the years."

The host families went to great lengths to please their American guests. For example, Americans reputedly had large appetites to fill with quantities of delicate Japanese food. "I did not like Japanese food," Craig Sherman '85 recalls. "Of course, the last thing I wanted was for my host family mother to think I didn't like her food, so I smiled and told flat-out lies.... I'd shovel my food down without pause, without chewing if possible, always praising her cooking. Of course, my host mother concluded that I had a bigger appetite than even she had thought, and she started to cook more food and insist on giving me seconds...." Sherman, who would later live in Japan, eventually learned that his host mother was a wonderful cook.

Nakajima advised, mentored, and befriended the SPS boys and girls for over twenty years. Every American uniformly sang his praises. He met them at the airport, and rode his bicycle around, watching his charges at school, at host homes, and at off-hours activities. He might call in the evenings on any pretext to find out how things were going. He felt pride and relief when his foreign charges successfully negotiated some Japanese challenge.

Seikei had a surprise for the early American students. They were asked to stand before the school faculty and student body, 1,500 strong, politely formed in rows, and give a speech—in Japanese! Eventually, the "visitor students" were given time to prepare. This public speaking strained their abilities and nerves, but each

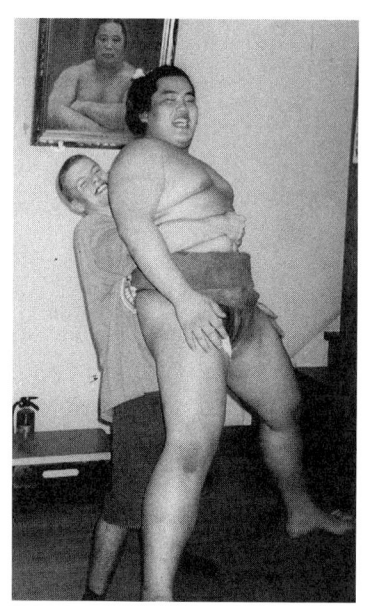

Timothy Ferriss tackles sumo wrestling, 1994.

Craig Sherman tucks in to Japanese food, 1985.

of them managed and each received polite applause (and perhaps scattered giggles). All exchange students sweated through it: "Through this procedure they are enabled to firmly establish their presence among us soon after joining the school," explained Nakajima.

American students participated in Seikei's extracurricular activities. Several joined music groups where their classmates expected them to know American rock and roll songs—and to sing them. Craig Sherman was the lead singer in a Seikei school rock band that played at the *bunkasai* (culture festival). "My fellow band members were quick to point out why I got picked as the lead singer—we were singing all U.S. and British pop music and I had the best English accent in the school!" Instrumental lessons were available. Tara McGowan "took private classes in *shakuhachi* [Japanese bamboo flute], traditional dance, tea ceremony, and flower arrangement and was allowed to continue my study of Western transverse flute with a Japanese teacher."

Both boys and girls wanted to experience unique Japanese sports. *Kendo*, a mock sword battle with a bamboo stick, seemed to be a favorite. Timothy Ferriss '95, Caroline Kenney '91, McKee, and Bentel all remembered *kendo* in physical education classes and some of them competed in tournaments. Ferriss "especially gave his all when it came to judo practice," wrote the exchange coordinator, impressed when Ferriss won a judo contest.

Seikei offered basketball, swimming, track, soccer, and tennis. "On my first day of practice," says Joshua Brooks, "I 'dunked' a basketball, which none of the other students had seen in person before. At the next day's practice there was a sizable group of students in the gym who chanted 'dunk, dunk, dunk...' every time I took the ball. Unfortunately, in my attempts to impress all I could manage was to dribble the ball off my knee several times in a row."

On vacations the Americans explored Japan. Seikei sponsored school trips for its students. One trip took in the ancient capital Kyoto and the sacred Nara. The foreign students were welcome to go along, for the standard cost. All did; the great historic castles and shrines of imperial Japan were not to be missed. McGowan went to *yama no gakko* (mountain climbing school) to prepare for a climb to the top of Mt. Fuji: "I also went on a student trip in the summer [to]...*Eiheiji*, a [Zen] Buddhist temple where we were taught how to sit in meditation and were served the vegetarian 'priest's food.'"

Caroline Kenney and her host father, Masuo Kashihara, 1991.

Often host families took the SPS scholars off to see sights and visit recreational facilities. Exchange coordinator Nakajima worried when he did not know where they were. To Nakajima's distress, McGowan traveled alone around Kyushu for a week. Nakajima made her give him an itinerary so he could call every night. "I remember having to pass up a tempting invitation to stay at an early Edo-period villa with a kind elderly woman I met in passing, only because I knew Nakajima-*sensei* would be calling the youth hostel somewhere else that night, or having to hitch a ride with a traveling music troupe through the mountains when I missed a connection, just to get to the next accommodation in time for that call." McGowan came to appreciate his parental-like concern. "I wandered around Nagasaki for three hours in a daze after reading final farewell letters from atomic bomb victims and winding up in a completely unfamiliar part of the city,... I appreciated hearing his voice."

When the Seikei year was over, some of the Americans returned home, others took the opportunity to travel more. For all of them, the experience of "being foreign" made a lasting impact. As Tadaaki Shimizu, successor to Nakajima as exchange program coordinator, put it, the American student "...learned various kinds of things about Japan through the people he met, the places he visited, and the experiences he had. We feel sure that this experience will motivate him to study Japanese all the more and bring him back to Japan someday in the near future."

The 1995 Advanced Studies class gathers in St. Paul's gothic chapel, which is decorated for the occasion with origami and Japanese banners.

CHAPTER 6

'Ringing Loud'

The Advanced Studies Program

In 1956 Matthew Warren had appointed a ten-person commission to develop a program for using St. Paul's School's assets to benefit the larger New Hampshire community in which the school lives. This resulted in the Advanced Studies Program *(ASP)* to "provide talented high school students from New Hampshire public and parochial schools with challenging educational opportunities otherwise unavailable to them." For six weeks each July and August, beginning in 1957, the school's library, dorm, and athletic facilities were opened to selected students taking specialized courses. The faculty was recruited from SPS and other institutions. College students, many of whom were previous ASP and SPS graduates, helped as interns or assistant teachers. The ASP has enhanced the education of over 7,400 New Hampshire students.

When André Hurtgen returned in 1984 from his sabbatical year at the Seikei School, he believed that he could contribute to the program. "I felt there is so much to learn about Japanese culture, people, history, arts, crafts, etc., and therefore so much to teach." The ASP could be a perfect vehicle. Just as Kaori Kitazawa created the first Japanese language course in the winter school on the framework of an existing SPS program, so Hurtgen proposed a course on the framework of the existing ASP.

He titled it "An Introduction to Japanese Language and Culture." As the ASP catalog would later read, "The aim of this course is to explore the richness of the culture and language of the Japanese people, who have recently emerged as both valued friends and fierce competitors of this country." When Hurtgen submitted his proposal to the department heads for approval, Hurtgen got the impression that "my proposal was received with polite yet definite snickers and humpf-humpfs: What makes André think he is an expert on Japan?" Nevertheless, the humpf-humpfing heads passed his proposal, and he taught the course for the first time in the summer of 1985.

Of a surprising 70 applications, fifteen students were selected for the first Japanese ASP class. "Reasons for taking the course," Hurtgen later wrote, "went from 'wanting to try something completely different for a little while,' to 'being bored with Romance languages and looking for a challenge.' One student enrolled because he felt he 'would not be behind, hence inferior to, the others!'"

"As I was setting all this up," Hurtgen recalls, "I wrote to Takahiro Hiraoka (who had befriended me on my first visit to Japan in 1981 and had been a great support during my stay at Seikei) casually saying, 'You should come over and help me teach it!' Much to my surprise he agreed at once." So began annual Seikei teacher visits to St. Paul's School.

Seikei teachers had visited St. Paul's briefly before this, but they had not come to teach. The first was Mamoru Shimizu who toured SPS while visiting his son Yoshiaki at Harvard in 1958. In 1962, Hironori Hirata, a mathematics teacher and superb go player, looked in while on a tour of the United States for goodwill games with American go players. Masahiko Okuzumi celebrated the two schools' partnership at St. Paul's in 1980. Satoru Nakajima realized his wish and first saw SPS in 1983 while in the Boston area leading a summer home-stay group. He had missed an opportunity to see SPS in 1960 when he came to the United States on a Fulbright program for secondary school teachers.

Hiraoka, an English teacher with a master's degree in American and English literature, joined Hurtgen's first class for its last two weeks. "The two weeks that I spent at Millville in the summer of 1985," he says, "have become a proud part of my teaching career....

ASP students from New Hampshire public schools learn Japanese culture through language, arts and crafts.

A barrage of questions waited for me. I responded to each of them as plainly and intelligibly as possible with all my might—questions which ranged from the complicated writing system of Japanese to the economic problems of the day."

Making the most of his stay in "a culture totally different," Hiraoka visited sights of New England at every opportunity. This Japanese specialist in English and American literature particularly sought out nearby Walden Pond, Willa Cather's grave, and the homesteads of Emily Dickinson, Ralph Waldo Emerson, and Louisa May Alcott. He also toured colleges—Dartmouth, Harvard, Mt. Holyoke, Yale, and MIT.

Hiraoka met Christa MacAuliffe, the Concord school teacher who was to be the first civilian in space but was killed when the *Challenger* spaceship exploded. "It was on the evening of August 6, 1985, that I met her in the square in front of the State Capitol. Lots of people had got together to send her off to Houston with great enthusiasm. As soon as the ceremony came to an end, I approached her and said, "Good luck, Christa. I'm looking forward to hearing

Takahiro Hiraoka meets Christa MacAuliffe, the ill-fated astronaut, in 1985.

your lecture from space.' She smiled and kindly wrote me her autograph, adding 'Reach for the Stars!'"

Of his visit, Hiraoka says, "It was an amazing adventure into New England."

Each summer thereafter, a teacher from Seikei has flown to St. Paul's School for two weeks to help Hurtgen teach his class. After the first visitor, Seikei gave its teachers a stipend for the trip. Because of the academic calendar in Japan, teachers could arrive only about July 25. In 1994, Clark's successor, David Hicks, the tenth SPS rector, cut the ASP to five weeks, a move that shortened the Japanese visitor's time to one week.

"All of Takahiro's successors have been more 'official' in that they now also receive a stipend from Seikei in addition to that from the ASP," Hurtgen explained. "The first six years or so I did the selection by asking the Seikei principal if he would agree that so-and-so come over, but in recent years SPS had asked the Seikei principal to nominate the visitor. This is a better, more formal procedure; furthermore, all the teachers I knew personally have now been here. More recent participants have been young teachers who have joined Seikei since my time.... I must say, however, that all my visitors have been quite extraordinary in their ability to overcome or totally ignore or pretend to ignore jet lag, jump right into action as though they had been there all along, and, make a really powerful impression on the class."

Most of the visitors were English teachers, so language was not a problem. They attended chapel, ate with the students, cheered at the athletic contests, and otherwise totally experienced the ASP life. The public school students valued having a "real live Japanese" teacher. Takahiro Hiraoka later spoke for all the Seikei visitors to André Hurtgen's classes: "We, as his counterparts, willingly helped him to enrich his grand plan of building a bridge over the Pacific."

ASP student and intern Josh Hornik imagined what it must have been like for the visiting Seikei teachers: "You take an all-day plane trip, covering twelve hours of time zones. You're picked up at the airport by a crazy white-haired Belgian man speaking Japanese and whisked to Concord, New Hampshire. You are wakened early the next morning and, after an American breakfast at the Upper, seated in the chapel among 200 chattering ASP students. You are quickly singled out as the new Japanese guest [a horrible thing for an unassuming Japanese to bear]. In your honor, banners are unfurled, *haiku* mispronounced, and Japanese folklore Americanized. Finally you are toasted with a rousing, if atonal, version of the Seikei school song."

Hornik's imagination, while facetiously pointing out the strangeness of the experience, really belies the visiting teachers' true impressions. The chapel welcome, the scrolls, the origami, the folk tale skit, the talks, and the song have become traditional. Michiko Yamato, a Seikei English teacher, arrived in 1998: "We gathered at the chapel.... What impressed me then were several large Japanese calligraphy scrolls created by students who wrote, 'Welcome, Ms. Yamato,' 'Seikei-Gakuen,' 'Japanese class is No. 1,' and also a large amount of 'thousand origami paper cranes.' They had also practiced for me the 'Seikei School Song' and 'Hello, Friends,' [a Japanese popular song]. We all sang these songs in front of all participants of the program. One student made a welcome speech and explained to all the relationship between our two schools. Other students performed a mini-skit, which originated from the Japanese nursery tale, '*Obasute-Yama*.' I was amazed by their well-prepared performance. I was so happy when they sang the Seikei song that when I came back to Japan I told this story to my students."

Satoru Nakajima, the Seikei teacher who had been so helpful to the SPS students at Seikei, came to the ASP class in 1986. He was "struck by the continued enthusiasm of Mr. Hurtgen in the study of our language, remembering how he used to call it the 'devil's language.'" Speaking about the students nine years later, Seikei teacher Sayaka Atobe, who taught exchange students Japanese at Seikei, was

Michiko Yamato shows off a proud student holding his calligraphy—in his right hand a classical poem, in his left his own composition.

"surprised to know that they studied Japanese for the first time a couple of weeks ago." She thought "that André-*sensei* taught it to them using some special magic."

Before taking his class, most New Hampshire students had studied little or nothing about Japan. Movies and news clips may have been their only sources of information on Japan. Hurtgen's brand of "special magic" sparked his students. Shireen Meskoob, who took the course in 1998, remembers: "Hurtgen-*sensei* brought Japan to the classroom in myriad ways. He and Valerie-*san* [Valerie Minakawa, an intern] immersed our class into the language and culture by speaking Japanese from the very first day. We were bewildered and couldn't believe we may ever understand *sensei*. By the end of the five-week course, not only could we understand and speak Japanese, we were singing it; not only could we identify Japanese gardens and flower arrangements, we were making them; we wouldn't just look at beautifully detailed kimonos, we were wearing them; we weren't just imagining ourselves at a tea ceremony as we sat on our feet for a painful 40-some-odd minutes, we actually attended one in Boston; we didn't

Sayaka Atobe teaches and practices the ritual Japanese tea ceremony for the benefit of relaxed American students.

just dream about eating raw fish, some of us actually did, at the Tatsukichi Restaurant; and we didn't just [look at] works of Japanese calligraphy, we signed them as a professional Japanese artist would with our own seals we had made from a chunk of eraser and a carving knife."

The active teaching method worked wonders. "Throughout the course I teach the kids how to be Japanese: bowing in and out of class, sitting up straight in their chairs, never expressing disagreement in a forceful manner, etc., etc." The teacher himself was less formal, however. Katy Clark can't forget Hurtgen in 1993, "taking a nose dive onto the grass and jumping right back up again during our simulation of Japanese school relay races." Kristen Schade, two years later, recalls "Hurtgen-*sensei* hopping across the classroom as he taught us how to read an accent mark that gave a sort of 'jump' to a word as one spoke it."

In four weeks, by using a dictionary, the ASP students could read and write as many as 25 *kanji* with *hiragana* and *katakana* characters. Seikei teachers corrected the final Japanese language exams. "On the corrected exam she wrote thoughtful comments," remembered 1998 student, Jason Kidd.

In contrast to the required Japanese behavior in his class, Hurtgen tells his students to be "American" in their dealings with the visiting teachers. "For example, I encourage them to ask sharp questions about say, the inferior role of women, discrimination against *burakumin* [descendants of a once-outcast group] and Koreans, arranged marriages, etc., etc."

The visiting teachers did notice the American students' habits. Michiko Yamato wrote, "Their motivation and diligence impressed me and I had to admit that I had to change my previous opinion that Japanese students study hardest." Yamato compared American and Japanese students: "American students are much more positive in exploring what they find interesting to learn and they know how to develop their interests. They go to libraries, collect data, acquire the necessary information, think and discuss, then show and tell us what they have done. Japanese schools, on the other hand, ask students to master every academic field systematically and generally." After observing a science class presentation of independent projects, she respected the "high level of research.... American students are truly gifted when it comes to showing their individuality and performing in front of people." What impressed Nakajima most about the Japanese class "was the good manners of the students and their genuine interest in studying."

The teachers, in turn, impressed the American students. "She was energetic, enthusiastic, friendly, and fun," wrote Kara French about 1992 guest Sumiko Nakamura. "I remember some of my fellow classmates and I thought that she was the antithesis of everything we had learned that Japanese women were supposed to be: submissive, shy. So we all thought it was cool that she broke these stereotypes."

Sayaka Atobe also was "cool." One day she went to Big Turkey pond to see the crew practice. "Our coach let her ride along on the motorboat that she drove alongside us as we rowed," related student Kristin Schade. "After practice, as we were getting ready to lift the boats out of the water, our coach turned the motorboat around and sped off. Atobe-*sensei* threw her arms in the air, gave out a yell, and, laughing, clapped. She brought the same sort of enthusiasm and spirit to everything she taught us."

When Kara French and two friends needed help on their project on Japanese festivals, Sumiko Nakamura found them studying a book on Japanese holidays. The Japanese teacher looked at the book. "Nakamura-*sensei* just cracked up and couldn't stop laughing. At first we didn't understand why, but then she explained that she had never seen anything like that in her life."

The Seikei teachers treated their ASP students to many gifts and class projects: lacquer boxes, candy, chop sticks, fans, *geta* shoes (high wooden clogs). The visitors taught and demonstrated *ikebana* (flower arranging), *hanafuda* (gambling card games), *ojigi* (bowing technique), *daruma* dolls, *kendo,* and an endless variety of cultural and artistic subjects.

Each teacher emphasized personal favorites. "For one week Nihei-*sensei* taught us the Japanese art of calligraphy—and how a simple brushstroke had a world of meaning," Abigail Dunne recalled. Dunne had learned the uses and handling of the brush from Seikei calligraphy teacher Koichi Nihei who had met his American students at a "Moonviewing Party." Nihei "was deeply impressed and delighted to see the students making remarkable progress," when they wrote words of their own choice like "peace," "friendship," and "love." "I still have the calligraphy from that week," Dunne says, "as well as a piece that Nihei-*sensei* did for me symbolizing my favorite Japanese poem: 'A small pond. A frog jumps in. The sound of water.'"

Several teachers brought the Japanese card game *karuta*, a lotto-like game. Hiromi Takahashi used it as a language teaching tool. "On each card the latter half of a poem is written in *hiragana*. There are 100 poems altogether. We put the cards on the floor. There is a person who reads the poems aloud at random. Players have to find out which poem is being read, and the one that takes the cards the most wins the game."

Origami, the Japanese art of paper folding, was a favorite, but troublesome. "I was terrible at it," Jason Kidd confessed. "Despite the ugliness of the cranes that I made in class, Miss Yamato assured me that they were very well done." With Sayaka Atobe's help, "we performed a tea ceremony and she provided us with kimonos and all of the other necessary materials [e.g., tea, special cups, and stirring spoons], so that we could make the ceremony as realistic as possible." Atobe taught: "It is not only serving tea, but also serving sweets, decorating flowers, hanging scrolls on the wall, and choosing a cup, etc., for guests. They wrote in calligraphy class,... picked wild flowers for decorating, and tried to serve teas again and again. And I prepared sweets in the kitchen. Including me, the class enjoyed it well."

Several Seikei teachers found themselves humbled in teaching about Japanese culture. "I remember spending quite a bit of time in the afternoons and evenings preparing for the next day's lessons just as the students did, which I needed to do to keep up with the class," confessed Satoru Nakajima. "This may sound rather strange, as the level of Japanese the students were learning was quite rudimentary, but in matters relating to the Japanese culture, what they were doing was not necessarily so, and I was made to keenly realize how ill-prepared I was as an exponent of our own culture."

ASP taught the teachers, too. An unusually candid and perceptive Sayaka Atobe also felt ill-prepared, and her needs stimulated her: "When I'd like to tell them about Japan, I found that I felt myself impatient because I didn't know about it well, as almost all of Japanese did. We are not usually conscious that we are Japanese…but thanks to ASP, I realized that Japanese culture was great and I myself am more interested in it."

Through the ASP, Seikei has learned much about St. Paul's School. It is no longer a faraway institution presumed to be affiliated with Harvard University. The Japanese are getting to know better and better the 'real live' St. Paul's—dynamic, challenging, and beautiful—filled with variety, humor, and motivation. Seikei teachers have now known American adolescents, becoming better acquainted with their spirit, their motives, and their interests.

The teacher exchange must have helped the Seikei English teachers practice their English-speaking skills. And, as Hurtgen recognizes, "Indirectly, this benefits SPS students who go to Seikei, for they are no longer regarded quite as 'strangers from a strange land' as they used to be."

Hurtgen estimates proudly that well over 200 New Hampshire students have been exposed to Japanese culture during the fifteen years of the ASP "Introduction to Japanese Language and Culture" course. Of these students perhaps 30 or more decided to major in Asian or Japanese studies in college. Fifteen or more went on to study in Japan. Five returned to St. Paul's School as interns and then were selected to participate in the Japan Exchange Teachers program.

For over 40 years, Satoru Nakajima has been immeasurably valuable to St. Paul's' students and visitors in his kind, caring, and humble way. He reveals what he and André Hurtgen did together at St. Paul's School on ASP graduation day in 1986:

"On that day, the weather was beautiful, and we spent part of the morning doing some outdoor game, which ended up in our climbing to the top of the chapel. That was quite an experience. I have been to St. Paul's four times, but that was the only time I went up to the top of the chapel and commanded a fine view of the campus below us. But I remember the experience more because of one other thing we did. We took turns in ringing the chapel bells, in quite a haphazard way, and ding-dong-dong, the bells kept ringing loud and irregularly."

Japanese at St. Paul's

"[I]t took me nearly one year
before I started to make myself understood to my peers."

"I went into my room and I smelled shellac. Newly applied shellac on
the floor. That was something very odd. We don't see painted surfaces
in a Japanese interior... That was a wonderful smell.
Something strange, but something very intimate...."

"In Japan we are trained not to express ourselves, but rather to
feel with our group. In the United States, people are urged
to be themselves at all cost, sometimes with ludicrous results."

"When I face any difficulty, I say to myself, I can do it.
Nothing is more difficult than what I've been through at SPS."

"St. Paul's never made me feel homesick in spite of the loneliness I
felt at times when there were no ready made
and more familiar patterns of life to follow."

"St. Paul's School taught me the fundamental decency
of the American society."

Americans at Seikei

"I felt nothing but fright, and had questions bouncing off the walls
of my head such as, 'Are you crazy?'"

"Looking out over a sea of meticulous blue uniforms
all I could think of was how clearly I did not fit in."

"By the end of the year at Seikei I...had difficulty
responding immediately when posed a question in English.
This kind of immersion learning is emotionally
and psychologically very stressful."

"My first boy friend was Japanese."

"I remember being very lonely and frightened...
They tried their best to make me feel at home,
but everything was so foreign and at first uncomfortable!"

CHAPTER 7

'In Honor of Those'

The Nineties

In 1988 André Hurtgen had given a talk to form representatives for annual giving to St. Paul's. He advocated a "Fund for International Studies" to encourage SPS students to study abroad, to foster exchanges of students and teachers, and to award books and prizes. He noted that there were prizes for dead languages, and for traditional European languages, but "we have no prize for the top student in Chinese or Japanese."

In Hurtgen's audience sat Haven N. B. Pell '64, who soon became a major player in a drive to raise money for the Japanese program. Pell was moved to fund a prize. The formal acknowledgment would recognize the exchange program's longevity and accomplishment. In 1990, SPS awarded the first St. Paul's-Seikei Japanese Prize to Julian Jiro Wimbush, whose mother was Japanese. Wimbush would study at Seikei, hold an internship at Mitsubishi, and do research in the East China Sea before entering Brown University.

Since then, this prize has been given annually "in honor of those who have encouraged or participated in the exchange of students between the two schools, to the student chosen by the language division, on the basis of grades, classroom performance, and participation."

The Japanese St. Paul's-Seikei alumni have gathered socially in Tokyo for years. They originally called themselves the "SPS-Seikei Club." Every year they would throw send-off parties for departing students. Those living or studying in the United States frequently met the new students and helped them adapt to their new surroundings. Americans were always welcomed in Tokyo, too, and visits of SPS faculty and graduates made occasions for socializing.

On June 29, 1990, to celebrate the schools' 40-year association, the St. Paul's and Seikei alumni associations sponsored a cocktail party in Tokyo. More than 50 students, graduates, parents, and friends—some traveling from as far as Washington and Hong Kong—came to celebrate the anniversary.

It had become evident that many Japanese and American SPS alumni who did not attend Seikei lived and worked in Japan. Increasing cultural exchanges between Japan and America brought more and more SPS graduates to Japan. In January 1991 on the occasion of a gathering of SPS-Seikei alumni in Tokyo to welcome W. Walker Lewis, then chairman of St. Paul's board of trustees, Minoru Makihara announced that the SPS-Seikei Club should not thereafter limit its membership to Seikei alumni but should accept everyone who attended SPS and wished to join the club.

A new club was formed, called the "SPS Club of Japan," with Makihara its chairman and Tatsuo Arima '53, Haven Pell '64, Sekison Lu '67, and Kiyoshi Matsumi '71 as other officers. The new club is now a contact point for an instant network for all SPS alumni in Japan. It was the first SPS alumni club formed outside the United States.

The Japanese alumni also acted to raise money. Makihara believed that St. Paul's had given much to the Japanese—40 years of scholarships—and that it was appropriate for the Japanese to make a contribution. Under his leadership, the alumni undertook to raise money to support the relationship. The purpose of the fund would be not to replace programs already existing but to supplement them with new initiatives such as faculty exchanges, student exchanges, and purchases of educational materials.

In September 1990 a fundraising campaign began in both Japan and America. Thirty-eight Japanese and 36 Americans contributed. The Mitsubishi Estate (USA) made a large gift. In less than six months, the "Fund for Japanese Studies" at St. Paul's had reached its goal.

N o custom at SPS is more enduring than that of carving the name of every student into the paneling in Coit Hall. Some families have graduated three and four generations of SPS students and their names appear repeatedly in the carving. On one of his many visits to SPS, Yoshiaki Shimizu showed his children his permanently recorded name. "As I visited the Chapel and the classrooms, and gazed and touched my name amidst ninety some others carved on a walnut panel of the wall,...I felt a new energy surging within me, and I sensed, this time with my children milling around me, the beginning of a new life cycle."

One of the children "milling around" Shimizu that day grew up to become the first descendent of a Seikei scholar to graduate from St. Paul's. Shimizu's daughter, Karen Akiko Marie, joined SPS in the Fourth Form. Like her father, Karen was an artist. "What interests me most is representations that aren't exactly realistic and are more drawn from my imagination," Karen told the *SPS Pelican*. She selected art for the *Horae Scholasticae* and published her own pulsating pastel figures and charcoal sketches. In 1998 Karen Shimizu graduated *magna cum laude*, with distinction in art and humanities.

Karen is now studying at Smith College. "As a career, art on its own could very well leave me, in the grand tradition, an empty stomach. I might look into art history," Karen mused before choosing to major in American studies. Karen's grandfather is Mamoru Shimizu, the Japanese professor who, with Henry Kittredge, had started the Seikei program 50 years ago. Three generations have shaped the first Seikei legacy at St. Paul's. A "new life cycle" has indeed turned.

In her father's footsteps at SPS: Karen Akiko Shimizu '98.

The Right Reverend Craig B. Anderson, eleventh rector of SPS, made his first visit to Tokyo in March 1998. The alumni welcomed the

Andersons at a reception at the Global House. Mamoru Shimizu, "trailblazer of this program," gave the traditional toast. Anderson gave special gifts to those who had contributed to the program—Makihara, Arima, Yokochi, M. Shimizu, Nakajima, and Tanioka. Makihara "expressed his desire to make this school-to-school relationship develop into something which can symbolize globalization in the future."

The 50th anniversary of the schools' relationship—by then some were calling it a partnership—was coming. Arima and Makihara wanted to do something memorable at the half-century mark. An idea took shape: The Emperor of Japan would award a decoration to a person who had been at St. Paul's when Makihara arrived 50 years earlier. They set in motion the necessary official machinery to honor St. Paul's through its rector emeritus, William Oates.

Oates had been a member of the admissions committee that admitted the first Seikei scholar to SPS. He had been the director of admissions who year after year had greeted Seikei scholars at the Concord station and the vice rector under whom the first Americans attended Seikei. He was rector when the Japanese language programs began, and the rector emeritus who had been the first to visit Seikei.

On June 2, 1999, the Japanese consul general invited Oates, his wife Jean, his three sons, SPS Rector Anderson, Mrs. Anderson, and several friends to a ceremony and luncheon at his residence near Boston, Massachusetts. Consul General Sinichi Kitajima bowed deeply to the 82-year-old educator. Then he presented a 24-inch square Japanese scroll with the official Japanese Seal of State, signed by Prime Minister Keizo Obuchi and Director General of Decoration Mokoto Sakaki. An imperial messenger had carried the award from Tokyo to Boston for this moment.

Kitajima reverently read the citation in Japanese. Then he translated: "His Majesty the Emperor of Japan has conferred on William Armstrong Oates this Imperial Decoration dated April 29, 1999, the Order of the Sacred Treasure,

Julian Wimbush, first SPS-Seikei prize winner, 1990.

Honored by the Emperor of Japan, Rector Oates accepts his citation in Boston, 1999.

Gold Rays with Neck Ribbon, in recognition that Oates started this famous and useful exchange program between St. Paul's School and Seikei Gakuen."

The consul general stepped behind Oates and hung the decoration around his neck. The gold rays shone from Oates' chest as the smiling rector emeritus spoke. "Mr. Kitajima, I want to thank you very much. I want to thank those who have come a distance to be here, from New Jersey, California, Massachusetts, New Hampshire, a representative group of that country of which I'm a citizen. I was one of several who participated in the start of the SPS-Seikei program. In the beginning a minor part. Mr. Kittredge had the most significant idea and having the hope and the vision of a program starting modestly and growing important. David Pyle had the yearning that something be done, and the significant assent of the entire faculty and of the school wanting to go forward."

Rector Anderson, representing St. Paul's, thanked Kitajima, the representative of the Japanese people, "For your honoring him, we feel honored as well," he declared. An exquisite five-course luncheon followed.

"The ceremony was simple and direct, in one sense humbling and in another much appreciated," Oates later said. "The honor shone through me to the school and lots of other people. It was accepted as part personal and in enormous part an institutional recognition. It has to be seen as a generous and important step by the Japanese gov-

Craig Anderson, eleventh rector of St. Paul's School, chats with Tatsuo Arima at a reception in Tokyo, 1998.

ernment and country recognizing this massive 50-year program."

In September and October of the last year of the 20th century, St. Paul's-Seikei alumni and friends celebrated the partnership's 50th anniversary with reciprocal all-day parties. A St. Paul's delegation jetted to Japan for Seikei's reception and banquet on September 21, 1999. Bishop and Mrs. Anderson were joined by André Hurtgen, William R. Matthews, Jr., executive director of the SPS Alumni Association, Mrs. Matthews, and Katherine Hardy, SPS director of development.

In the morning the delegation visited Seikei. To the accompaniment of thunder from skies threatening rain, Rector Anderson addressed the assembled High School student body. Yoshiaki Shimizu's younger brother, Taadaki Shimizu, Seikei's coordinator of foreign exchanges, translated his words. Not until he finished did the thunder clap along with the students, and the skies open. The SPS delegation fled indoors, where Seikei High School principal Takashi Yokochi offered a light lunch; then the delegation met Seikei teachers in the faculty room and spoke with the Japanese educators.

That evening, the Asuka Room of the Century Hyatt Hotel, Shinjuku, Tokyo, opened to 60 friends and alumni for a buffet banquet that Hurtgen called "lavish and elegant." The school leaders opened the congratulatory speeches; everyone toasted the schools' mutual friendship. After the buffet, guests heard more speeches from Mamoru Shimizu, Minoru Makihara, Robert A. G. Monks, Satoru Nakajima, and André Hurtgen.

After the party paused for more "lavish and elegant" food, individual gifts were exchanged among the American and Japanese guests. Rector Anderson presented to Seikei a Tiffany silver tray engraved with the seals of the two schools and the words: "St. Paul's-Seikei 1949–1999 Fifty Years of Friendship." Alumni Miki Tanaka '84 and Craig Sherman '85 addressed the guests. The evening ceremonies closed grandly when the vice grand master of ceremony for the Japanese emperor addressed the celebrants. This speaker was SPS-Seikei graduate Motoi Okubo '59.

A month later, on October 22, St. Paul's reciprocated the anniversary festivities in a day of activities planned by André Hurtgen. The campus was decorated with the last of the red and yellow autumn leaves, Hargate Hall exhibited works by ceramic artist Jun Kaneko, and the Ohrstrom Library displayed archives depicting the SPS-Seikei history.

The celebration began in early morning chapel, where the student body and guests heard a Buddhist scripture reading from *Kokoro No Chikara* (The Power of the Soul), the Seikei book of meditations: "Nature, she is our friend. The rustling, is it the sound of the wind? The roaring, is it the voice of the waters? The roaring is the song of earth; the rustling is the music of heaven...." Everyone then sang *"In Christ There Is No East or West...."*

Students in SPS's Japan Society stretched Seikei Principal Yokochi's gift, two brilliantly colored *koinobori*, or carp streamers that resemble flying windsocks, the length of the nave. Yokochi explained that these are traditionally flown on Japanese holidays to symbolize the growth of young people. Ben Makihara spoke, recalling the scripture: "I was a stranger and you took me in," and interpreting anew the Seikei motto: "Respect will come not from one's words, but from one's virtues."

The highlight of the day was a symposium on U.S.-Japan relations in the 21st century. The two powerful nations are searching for roles in the world. Both countries face new kinds of economic, political, and pedagogical realities. As Richard Ellings, director of the National Bureau of Asian Research, recently said, the U.S.-Japan relationship "is more important now than it was before the end of the Cold War."

The school assembled late in the morning at Memorial Hall to hear the experts discuss the future. Nicholas Platt '53, former U.S. ambassador to Zambia, the Philippines, and Pakistan, and currently president of the Asia Society, moderated. He noted that the very first instance of U.S.-Japanese security cooperation was when he and Tatsuo Arima as football teammates cooperated to "knock down their opponent." Then the first three Seikei scholars, who each have reached world prominence in their chosen careers, were joined by Professor Ezra Vogel, the director of the Fairbanks Center for East Asian Research at Harvard, whom Arima and Shimizu had tutored; by Akira Iriye, professor of American history at Harvard and Arima's Seikei classmate; and by Akari Yamaguchi '89, an international trade consultant. This panel, whose time was limited by the SPS student class schedule, spoke of the future. The talks highlighted the two countries' economic impact on the world, their common commitment to the values of liberal democracy, and optimism about their future relations. Makihara, chairman of Mitsubishi Corporation, characterized the United States and Japan as "pragmatic" countries engaged in "mega-competition" while at the same time with their combined strength benefiting others by their cooperation. In the talks, and in answers to questions, the panelists discussed how Japan and the United States still have much to learn about each other and that educational systems, especially the Japanese, need to prepare people to deal with innovation and change.

An evening banquet for nearly 100 alumni, friends, and school officials was served in the new hockey building. During dinner, congratulatory speeches continued, and Rector Anderson and Principal Yokochi liberally distributed gifts, while the guests enjoyed their meal. Later, former rectors Oates and Clark spoke about the constant SPS-Seikei friendship during the changes that had occurred in the schools and the world over the 50 years. The day concluded with another look at the future.

A prescient event had occurred in the morning—Bishop Anderson had received the following e-mail message from Japan:

"Sir Rector of St. Paul's School: My name is Satoshi Takagi, a first-grade student of Seikei High School in Japan. I am the webmaster of the international website and an international executive committee member of Leonids '99. Leonids '99 is the project to observe [the] Leonids meteor showers by high school students all over the world. I would like your school to take part in this project. So I wish you to visit our website."

Tagaki probably cannot imagine the two-month journey that 50

Celebrating 50 years of partnership, celebrants unfold a gift from Seikei on the SPS Chapel steps. From left: Takeshi Morita '01, Tatsuo Arima '53, Minoru Makihara '50, Akira Iriye, Yoshiaki Shimizu '55, Rector Anderson, Seikei Principal Takashi Yokoshi.

years ago was necessary before Japanese and American students could work together. But when his e-mail was read, he gave the anniversary celebrants a glimpse of the St. Paul's and Seikei partnership's future: students working together on study projects, becoming e-pen pals, sharing information, helping each other in instant electronic communication.

Pioneers: Tatsuo Arima, Minoru Makihara and Yoshiaki Shimizu, the three original Seikei scholars, pose together for the first time in four decades during the 50th anniversary year, Tokyo 1999.

CHAPTER 8

'How Great the Rewards'

The Graduates

Henry Kittredge had conceived his generous idea to bring foreign students to St. Paul's School as a way to teach American boys to understand other nations. In 50 years, 38 Seikei scholars have attended St. Paul's, including two that will graduate in the 21st century. Twenty-four St. Paul's scholars have attended Seikei in the 23 years since Stephen Vaskov '76 first set foot on its campus. Fifteen Seikei teachers have taught 225 Americans at the SPS Advanced Studies Program. An SPS teacher has taught hundreds of young Japanese at Seikei School and University.

Kittredge believed that individual friendships made early among people of different cultures would increase understanding among nations. As André Hurtgen has said, "Understanding a foreign culture is hard work. It takes time, dedication and an open mind. To begin to acquire such understanding is indeed a challenge for a 16-year-old. Living and studying in a different culture is arduous, even painful. But how great the rewards: new friends, broader visions, expanded opportunities, an added dimension to life and, in the long run, a better world."

Mamoru Shimizu, who selected the first three Japanese boys for St. Paul's, Makihara, Arima, and Shimizu, had written to Kittredge in

1954: "I believe that those three boys will, in the future, do something in the way of strengthening the tie between your country and ours so far advanced by your generous idea." The promise implicit in Henry Kittredge's generous idea was there from the beginning. As Makihara said 50 years ago: "From among the boys [and girls] of this school we shall see diplomats, politicians, and statesmen appear, and I believe all of you will become active members of this democratic society."

"St. Paul's and Seikei celebrate a growing list of distinguished 'alumni' of this exchange program which represents a modest but significant contribution to international understanding, relations, and peace," wrote Kelly Clark, the ninth SPS rector, in 1985. In 1999, 24 American and Japanese SPS-Seikei graduates are in business, six of them in media-related jobs, most in international positions taking them abroad. Six have entered academia, four law, four medicine, and two have careers in diplomacy. Fourteen are college or graduate students, many studying international relations or East Asian disciplines.

The first Seikei scholar, Minoru Makihara, returned to Japan after graduating from Harvard in 1954 and has been an international businessman with the Mitsubishi *keiretsu* (corporations related by ownership or contract). Starting in the Marine Products Group selling fish, he quickly became the group's head, and then served Mitsubishi for two decades in various capacities in Tokyo, London, Seattle, Washington, and New York. In 1972 he ran Mitsubishi's office—said to be the first office of any Japanese firm in the United States—at Washington's Watergate complex, next door to the Democratic National Committee headquarters.

A decade later, Makihara became chief executive officer of Mitsubishi International Corporation, based in the United States. At this time Japan was inundating the United States with Mitsubishi, Sony, Toyota, Honda, Toshiba, and other companies' automotive and electronic products. Japanese real estate investors made spectacular purchases of landmark properties in the United States, from Rockefeller Center in Manhattan to Pebble Beach Golf Course in California. Makihara was instrumental in Mitsubishi's acquiring Aristech Chemical Company.

By 1992, the "quiet boy" from Seikei had become, in the words of The New York Times, a "polished, cosmopolitan international businessman." That year, Makihara was named president of Mitsubishi Corporation, one of the largest companies in the world and prominent among the many interlinked companies of the Mitsubishi *keiretsu*. The Times called Mitsubishi "the most famous of Japan's trading companies, which deal in everything from oil to dam-building and precious art to agricultural imports.... The appointment was widely interpreted here [in Tokyo] as an effort by Japan's most politically powerful business group to project a gentler English-speaking image to the world." Makihara, known outside Japan by his SPS nickname "Ben," commented at that time: "My background is very non-traditional, but I am a very traditional person, fairly Japanese in my thinking.... Some people go abroad a short time and come back very different. Others go abroad a long time and come back unchanged. I think that I am one of the latter."

Makihara is now chairman of Mitsubishi Corporation. He has recently added a directorship of IBM to his credentials. One of Japan's most prominent businessmen, he has accompanied his country's prime minister on international missions. In December 1998, with Japan's prime minister and others in a Japanese delegation, he dined with President Clinton.

He has maintained lasting academic friendships with, among others, his SPS classmate George Randolf Packard III, dean of the School of International Studies at Johns Hopkins University, and Edwin Reischauer, whom professor Akira Iriye called the single-most influential individual in the history of U.S.-Japanese relations. And Makihara taught Robert Monks, his SPS and Harvard friend, about Japanese business. "All during this period of time we have been involved in one form of business or another," says Monks, an international business consultant. "He was always available," says Makihara of Monks, to give "solace in times of difficulty," and "sound practical advice." Makihara continues, "He has been a most thoughtful and generous friend, and also a constant source of intellectual stimulation."

In addition to leading alumni support for the Seikei-St. Paul's partnership for 50 years, Makihara has maintained his connections with Harvard. In 1973, he generated a million-dollar gift from Mitsubishi to Harvard Law School for comparative legal studies. This was possibly the first gift from Japan to an American university. In 1977, while he was a Mitsubishi executive, Makihara attended the advanced management program at Harvard Business School and alumni elected him president of the Harvard Club of

Japan. With William Oates, he now helps raise money for Harvard.

Makihara has said that his "greatest achievement" was "my decision to apply to St. Paul's School in the U.S. It led to my going to Harvard, and that in turn enabled my career to take the path it has. It was a difficult decision to make when Japan was at its lowest ebb just after the war, but I am glad that I seized the opportunity."

The second Seikei scholar, Tatsuo Arima, holds Harvard bachelor's and doctoral degrees in government. While at Harvard he tutored and befriended two other students who were then learning Japanese: Ezra Vogel, future director of the John K. Fairbanks Institute of Asian Studies at Harvard, and Henry Rossovsky, who became a specialist in Japanese economics and dean of Harvard's faculty of arts and sciences, and now is university professor emeritus.

After ten years in the United States, Arima joined the Japanese Ministry of Foreign Affairs in 1961, rose steadily in rank, and held high-level assignments including director of personnel, director-general of the North American Affairs Bureau, and chief cabinet counselor for external affairs. Overseas, he served as director of the political department in Washington, consul general in San Francisco, ambassador to The Netherlands, and ambassador to the Federal Republic of Germany. He is the first Japanese to have reached ambassadorial rank without a degree from Tokyo University.

In 1977, U.S. diplomat Nicholas Platt, Arima's classmate at St. Paul's, was named head of the Japanese desk at the State Department in Washington. On learning this, the Japanese Foreign Ministry promptly posted Arima to Washington as director of political affairs at the Japanese embassy. For the next three years the two St. Paul's School football teammates, Arima and Platt, became the official government channel between the United States and Japan.

"To have Tatsuo in Washington with me now," Platt told SPS students in 1978, "working on a basic, vital element of the foreign policies of our countries, is to me a sort of miraculous linkage of the past and present…. Policy development with the Japanese government is another major task, and on political issues my office will have the major say. Here I will work quite closely with Tatsuo. On average, since I took this job in July, I've been on the phone with him once a day; when things are hot, maybe three, four times a day…. We're trying to keep the relationship healthy. We are trying to avoid frictions. We are trying to put out fires. We are trying to

Classmates ond diplomats Nicholas Platt and Tatsuo Arima in 1978, back at SPS a quarter-century later.

limit damage.... It's on an instant-communication basis.

"Another thing we do together is prepare for the visits to each other's capitals of the most extraordinary number of high-level people. Twenty-three congressional delegates visited Tokyo last year [1977]. We had 80 visitors from the Japanese Diet...." A cabinet minister of each country visits the other each month. Platt and Arima negotiated these visitors' agendas, meetings, briefings—all prepared weeks in advance.

Arima explained his role: "My primary responsibility is to follow both the domestic political trends in the United States and major foreign policy issues.... Finally we deal with the U.S. Congress.... It has become important for...[diplomats] to make sure the legislators do understand the positions, views, or sentiments of the Japanese government or the Japanese people."

During his visit to SPS in 1978, 25 years after graduating, Arima paused before a chapel plaque in memory of an alumnus killed over Guam in 1944. He revealed his thoughts: "I let this plaque symbolize the sufferings, or sorrows that millions of people...all over the world

'How Great the Rewards'

experienced during the war, and I let my brief experience at St. Paul's symbolize our ability to overcome them in a creative manner. The history of our association, the history of our relationships—that is, between the United States and Japan and between St. Paul's and Seikei since the war—testifies to this."

Arima now represents the Japanese government around the world, and is perhaps its most important advisor on foreign affairs. While in Germany in 1996, Arima impressed listeners when he candidly commended the way Germans had acknowledged responsibility for World War II better than the Japanese. Over the years he has written and spoken with deep sensitivity about the Japanese character and his country's relations with America and Europe, acting, says his friend Robert Monks, less like a Japanese diplomat and more like an informed person speaking the Japanese mind.

In addition to his diplomatic duties, he now counsels Makihara as a corporate advisor to Mitsubishi Corporation. And, having turned down tenure at Harvard earlier in his career, in 1999 he accepted an appointment as professor of government at Japan's Waseda University.

The third Seikei scholar that Professor Shimizu foresaw would strengthen the U.S.-Japan tie was his second son, Yoshiaki. "The years I spent in America since my graduation from St. Paul's have not always been smooth sailing," says Yoshiaki Shimizu. "Torn between art and scholarship, I left Harvard three times, and three times did Harvard re-admit me with generosity and understanding." While at Harvard Shimizu chanced to see the popular movie, *Breakfast at Tiffany's*. The movie's exaggerated portrayal of a ridiculous Japanese artist, a sign of not-always-latent American xenophobia, upset him deeply. But he persevered, found his calling in art, and made his home in the United States.

Shimizu earned his doctorate in art and archaeology at Princeton in 1974. After working elsewhere for a decade, he accepted a full professorship of Japanese art and archeology at Princeton, served two years as chairman of the Art and Archeology Department, and in 1992 was appointed to the august Marquand Professorship, established in 1883. Allan Marquand, a distinguished art historian and humanist, had founded the department, and was the first person to hold this chair. "The world is fraught with wonders," Shimizu wrote to the SPS *Alumni Horae*. Allan Marquand had graduated from St. Paul's School in 1870.

Although he had chosen to live in the United States and his four children were American citizens, Shimizu had felt no urgency to give up his Japanese citizenship. But as time went on, he encountered some professional limitations and learned that aliens are disadvantaged in estate planning. "As a resident alien for nearly three decades I was enjoying all the liberties and rights in this country except voting right," he says. "With citizenship, one feels more responsible for his rights." On July 23, 1999, Shimizu raised his right hand before the American flag and swore allegiance to his adopted country.

One day 33 years after his graduation from St. Paul's, a quietly proud Shimizu stood in the National Gallery of Art in Washington, D.C., under a gigantic banner of a Samurai horseman. The banner proclaimed in letters nearly as tall as Shimizu, "JAPAN The Shaping of Daimyo Culture 1185–1868." It announced an extraordinary exhibit of nearly 500 works of Japanese art, many of which had never before left Japan.

In 1982 the National Gallery of Art had asked Shimizu to organize an exhibition of the art, artifacts, and culture of the Daimyo civilization. Working for over six years as guest curator, he drafted "wish lists" of objects, arranged for permits and permissions, organized the exhibit, wrote the book-length exhibition catalogue, and crossed the Pacific several times. The head of the team at Japan's *Bunchako* (the Agency for Cultural Affairs) responsible for approving the selections was a Seikei alumnus whom Shimizu had known from school days. "That kind of thing helped," Shimizu says. So did the fact that one of the chief private lenders of objects was another Seikei alumnus. The translator of the catalogue was another.

From October 1988 through January 1989, Shimizu's exhibition presented an illustrious period of Japanese history and culture to over 280,000 visitors from around the world. The Daimyo period's feudal lords and Samurai (warriors), headed by a Shogun, governed through a seven-century period of peace. Much of the East Building of the National Gallery was given over to the art and artifacts of a culture from half the world away and centuries ago: the eight-foot image of Amida, the Buddha, Shinto gods of nature, Samurai armor, silk robes adorned with flowers. A teahouse had been dismantled, flown from Kyoto, and reconstructed on the ground floor. On the walls hung priceless poetry and calligraphy, delicate ink paintings of cranes and tigers, bamboo groves and pine trees, and mountains—masterpieces all. It was as spectacular and precious a group of art objects as had ever before left Japan, many of the works designated "national treasures."

"It was at St. Paul's that my interest in art was kindled." Shimizu says. "The art teacher, Mr. Abbe, was the person who opened my eyes to art, and for that I am ever grateful to him, and to the school. Had it not been for the setting of St. Paul's and warm human contacts I was privileged to enjoy, I would not have chosen the life I am enjoying as an art historian."

Seikei Professor Mamoru Shimizu had foreseen that the three original Seikei scholars would "do something by way of strengthening the tie between your country and ours." He also must have believed that their successors, and others who entered the St. Paul's Seikei relationship, would also "do something." A review of some of those who followed those three exemplifies the men and women who, each in a unique way, have proved that Henry Kittredge's generous idea has, indeed, advanced.

Amy Nobu '78, who had spurred SPS students to start going to Seikei, felt that SPS's independent study program was "almost too creative for what I had been used to in the rather rigid Japanese educational system." But her project took her to work at the Concord Hospital, giving her "aspirations to become a physician eventually." She completed her education at Albany Medical College in 1986, entered family practice in northern Virginia, spent a year with an American embassy health unit in Tanzania, and returned to her family practice group in 1995.

"I elected to use my bicultural educational experience in a profession that may allow me to help fill the gap that exists between the two countries," Kaoruhiko Suzuki '67 has written. "I became a lawyer, specializing in U.S.-Japan business transactions." After Harvard Law School, he joined Paul, Hastings, Janofsky and Walker, a California firm. "As such, I encounter almost on a daily basis difficulties in maintaining meaningful communications across the Pacific and across cultural barriers. Language is certainly a problem but it can be and is overcome. A more fundamental difficulty is a failure to recognize that people tend to see the same set of facts from different

Amy Yoshiko Nobu '78, now a family physician, with sons Masaru and Sigeru, 1999.

viewpoints. The fable of six blind men describing an elephant in six different ways is an appropriate fable to describe the situation. What makes this difficulty worse is that each 'blind man' tends to believe that his perception is the correct one."

Hachiro Nakamura '61 remained in the United States after graduating from medical school at the State University of New York at Buffalo. "[SPS] was a superb, but almost surreal, educational experience," Nakamura believes. "As a cardiologist in private practice, I see patients of all different racial and cultural backgrounds, including some Japanese.... I have met people from the rest of America, from the most wealthy to the poorest, from the best educated to the near-illiterate—people of all different colors and religions, and I began to realize how surprisingly similar human nature is despite wide differences in cultural, social, financial, and physical backgrounds."

The Seikei experience inspired Americans, too, to live and work halfway around the globe from home. Craig Sherman '85 now lives in Tokyo, having fallen in love with Japan on a visit when he was thirteen years old. He had graduated from Princeton with a degree in East Asian studies, then worked for seven years for Cendant Corporation, a holding company for Coldwell Banker Real Estate, Avis car rental, motel chains such as Days Inn, Travelodge, and Howard Johnson, and related financing companies. In early 1996 Cendant's president asked him to sit in on a meeting with Uny, a Japanese company. "I sat in and found myself correcting the interpreter...." Soon he was in charge of establishing a joint venture with Uny and Mitsubishi called Cendant Japan. "Eighteen months later I was asked to move to Tokyo and run the small joint venture."

"I eventually majored in East Asian studies at college, which in turn provided me with the opportunity to study in Kyoto," wrote Sarah McCrum, a 1991 ASP student from a small New Hampshire town. "The reason why I am writing this here at my desk in the International Affairs Division in Oita Prefecture, Japan, is directly related to my decision eight years ago to take the 'Introduction to Japanese Language and Culture' course." In August [1999] I will end my job as coordinator for International Relations with the Japanese government and begin a new life here as a citizen married to a Japanese!"

The first American boy to attend Seikei for a full year, Charles McKee, Jr. '83 lived from 1993 to 1997 in Tokyo, running Virgin Atlantic Airways in Asia. He recalls: "While in Tokyo I had occasion to attend the Seikei Transportation Club, dedicated to alumni working in transport. It was great to see so many classmates in the same field of work—15 years older!" Now he is general manager for global distribution at Virgin Atlantic Airways, living in London and hoping to return to Tokyo where his children were born.

André Hurtgen has said that "cultural understanding takes an open mind." The panelists at the 50th anniversary symposium said, without dissent among them, that the Japanese educational system needs to and will produce students able to cope with innovation and not to fear mistakes. Many Seikei students had come to America expressly to "broaden horizons," and student after student has reported that St. Paul's had "opened their minds."

The SPS-Seikei partnership taught its open-minded students to follow interests in international affairs all over the world. A recent graduate, Shunsuke Okano '97, believes that it has traditionally been difficult to study international relations in Japan. "My most favorite [SPS] class was the history class about the Vietnam War with Mr. Green. It was not only because of the knowledge I learned in that class, but because of people's willingness to accept the unknown side of their own history, which we don't do in Japan." For mastering study in a foreign land Okano received the Schlager Prize for Valor at SPS, as the student most exhibiting courage, strength of character, and a determination to succeed. He now is an international relations major at Tufts University.

Motoi Okubo '59 graduated from Harvard with a degree in government. After further study at Kyoto University, he entered the Japanese Ministry of Foreign Affairs. For 30 years, including his time at the Ministry of Justice in Tokyo, Okubo has represented the Japanese government in Australia, Mexico, France, Bangladesh, Belgium, Jamaica, and the United States. He is now working on the Japanese imperial household staff as vice-grand master of ceremony.

Junko Watanabe '86 was inspired to teach math in Africa. Speaking of her SPS math teacher Timothy Howell, she says, "His attitudes towards math and students made me think that I also want to meet people all over the world by teaching math." For two years, Watanabe taught in a remote Kenyan village that had no money for books, teachers, or classrooms. She learned how the villagers worked hard, communicated, valued families, and enjoyed their own lives. "After the experiences of Kenya, I started to realize that no matter rich or poor, no matter where one lives on the globe, one has the challenge to find his own way of living."

Kiyoshi Matsumi Kikyo '71, an active supporter of the SPS-Seikei alumni groups in Japan, majored in chemistry at Trinity College, in Connecticut, and studied management for a master's degree at Northwestern University. Then he built a career at Mitsubishi, working in Tehran and Ho Chi Minh City, as well as in Tokyo.

Michiyuki Nagasawa '91 had already lived in Moscow when he returned to Seikei and in 1988 wrote a research paper predicting the end of the Cold War. Then he applied to St. Paul's so he could observe global relations from an American viewpoint. The Cold War ended shortly after he arrived at SPS. "I will never forget an SPS faculty [member], Mr. Lawrence S. Braden. In the class of calculus he taught us three points which altered my life," Nagasawa remembers. "The pleasure of solving academic problems and developing various ideas on them…the importance of thinking by oneself…and that analyzing matters in the abstract is as powerful and profitable as studying those in the concrete." He returned to Japan after graduating from SPS, earned a degree from Kyoto University and a master's degree in law from the University of Tokyo Law School, and is now studying for his doctorate there. "I'm always thinking about justice and equity based on Braden's three points," he says.

"After graduating from SPS," says Yoko Nishikawa '90, "I took a year off and spent time in Tokyo, and then I went to Georgetown

[University] in 1991 and majored in international relations. During that time, I interned at the Japanese embassy in Washington, D.C., and at CNN." In 1996 she started work for Reuters in Tokyo, focusing on economic and financial news. "I mainly cover news conferences at the Finance Ministry, the Economic Planning Agency, and the Bank of Japan, etc. And I now write and report in English!" But Nishikawa is more interested in people who make things or help others. She confesses, "It's a scary thought that news delivered by a person like me can move financial markets and let people gain or lose huge amounts of money in a matter of minutes."

The first American woman to study at Seikei, Elisabeth Bentel '83, majored in East Asian Studies at Harvard, spent her junior year in Japan, and after graduating returned to Tohoku University on a Fulbright Scholarship. She started work as an investment banker at Goldman Sachs. "Although Japanese language ability was nice on my résumé, I was not hired because of it. But...before I knew it, I was using it. The Japanese were hungry for U.S. real estate in the '80s, so after six months of mergers and acquisitions work, I found myself working exclusively on enormous real estate sales and financing in New York and Los Angeles for which practically all of the clients were Japanese."

Bentel studied law at Colum-

Yoko Nishikawa '90, now a Reuters correspondent, and Elisabeth Bentel Carpenter '83, broadcasting executive, 1999.

A GENEROUS IDEA

bia, clerked with a Japanese law firm, then studied business at Harvard. There she became interested in television and interactive media and eventually landed work at British Sky Broadcasting in London. "What possible use could [my Japanese experience] possibly be to me in the United Kingdom? Well, sure enough, it only took a year before I received a phone call from Rupert Murdoch himself asking me to go to Japan to evaluate a potential business opportunity there called JSkyB. The funny thing was that he did not even know that I spoke Japanese when he asked me. That conversation commenced an eighteen-month commute between London, New York, and Tokyo to start the new business now known as SkyPerfecTV, a joint venture between Sony News Corporation and FujiTV, among others."

St. Paul's-Seikei graduates have entered academia at all levels to "do something" with their bicultural interests. Tara McGowan '84 majored in comparative literature and East Asian studies at Princeton, and spent a year at the Inter-University Center for Japanese Language Study at Yokohama. While in Japan, McGowan edited and translated the 1983 nine-volume *Kodansha Encyclopedia of Japan*, a definitive cultural and historical encyclopedia of the country. For the next several years, she studied at Princeton and in Japan, on a grant from the Ito Foundation, learning about Japanese naturalist Kumagusu, and working as a translator.

McGowan married Princeton professor Richard Okada, who had taught Japanese at SPS. Their son was born in Kyoto and she is teaching him to respect his dual heritage. "On my return to Princeton, I became involved with the Japanese community there and helped to organize a 'home school' with a group of mainly Japanese mothers to teach our children Japanese.... I began to immerse myself and my son in Japanese folk tales as they are presented to children in Japan." She is the vice president of the PTA at the community Japanese Language School and many of her friends come from the Japanese community there.

"I am often called upon to explain or interpret culturally confounding situations," says McGowan, "whether it is a question of launching a new product in an unfamiliar cultural context or counseling a transferred family to deal with the daily trauma of functioning in a different country. Cultural advising has proven an expedient and inexpensive preventative measure.... My Seikei experience continues to enrich and influence my life up to the present moment."

Crystal Brunelli followed her St. Paul's 1989 summer introduction to Japan with a year abroad at the Stanford Japan Center in Kyoto. She recalls SPS: "In class, [Seikei visiting teacher] Mrs. Minami would clap her hands quietly and say "*subarashii*" (wonderful) after any of us spoke. Later, when I taught Japanese at the Andover summer session, I praised my students the same way." Brunelli now lives in Japan, not far from Seikei.

Kristen Ray, an ASP student in 1985, teaches second grade in Seattle. "I also remember, still, basic Japanese words and facts about their history and culture," Ray relates. "This has all helped me tremendously. The Seattle School district…has created a Japanese language program for its elementary students. Our school is one of the few pilot schools. I often think of my ASP '85 summer experience when I am teaching Japanese!"

"Something of [Seikei teachers] Tsuneharu and Aiko Kobuta's good will and André Hurtgen and intern Margo Hamburger's more sustained exertions must have stuck with me," says Charo D'Etcheverry, who took the ASP course in 1988. "I began studying Japanese language as part of my international politics and economics major at Middlebury College, and three years later I found myself in Kyoto for two semesters."

After Middlebury, D'Etcheverry received a master's from Harvard and matriculated to the East Asia Studies Department at Princeton. The Japan Foundation and Princeton sponsored further studies in Kanazawa and Yokohama. Her current doctoral advisor is Richard Okada. "My current assignment [is] assistant-teaching a post-war Japanese society and culture course, while completing my Ph.D., a study of three examples of late Heian prose fiction." She had never heard of Heian prose fiction until "that summer back in St. Paul's library when I picked up a translation of *The Tale of Genji* [a classic 11th-century novel] because Mr. Hurtgen had said it was good…. None of this would have even drifted into my horizon of possibilities without that St. Paul's summer," she says. "Perhaps some time soon I may be teaching students of my own who first learned of Japan from ASP and its Seikei guests." In 1998 she joined a seminar on *The Tale of Genji* led jointly by Okada and Yoshiaki Shimizu. Hurtgen did not know that his former summer student had become a serious Japanese scholar, and neither D'Etcheverry nor Shimizu realized their SPS-Seikei ties. When the 50th anniversary celebrations began, the three connected.

The SPS-Seikei partnership works well beyond the school years. In 1991, William Oates, SPS rector emeritus and a popular figure among the graduates, was cochairman of the board of directors of the Eisenhower Foundation. When the foundation sought financing for a program to send fourteen police chiefs from large American cities to Japan, Oates turned to an SPS-Seikei friend. "At my request, Tatsuo Arima gave important support for the Eisenhower application to the Japan Foundation for Global Partnership, funded by Japan, and a substantial grant of $250,000 was made for the 'Japan-United States Police Exchange and Implementation Program.' The trip has had the effect of introducing community policing to American cities: the concepts of police as friend, police as fellow citizen, police as community leader. Through community policing, American officers have been increasingly effective in their work."

The SPS-Seikei men and women have unique bonds of understanding as well as effective networks. In the words of André Hurtgen: "Each is especially well qualified to explain and interpret the Japanese mind to Americans, and the American way to the Japanese." When Junko Watanabe Nakamura '86 lived in Michigan, her infant daughter fell sick. Unhappy with her local doctor's explanations, she called her St. Paul's friend, Ann Abraham, a family physician in Rhode Island. "Although we had not talked in almost ten years.... I felt that she knew about us so well and I knew she was a doctor I could trust." When Yoshiaki Shimizu needed guidance with a medical problem, he likewise found comfort in talking to cardiologist Hachiro Nakamura '61.

Today, somewhere in the world an SPS-Seikei graduate is reading a folk tale to a little boy, renting a Toyota in Tokyo, or dining with a diplomat. Another is reporting a shift in international trade, lecturing on late Edo art, or repairing a diseased heart. Henry Kittredge, Mamoru Shimizu, and Minoru Makihara each knew that good results would come of young American and Japanese people becoming friends.

Mamoru Shimizu's prophetic words to Henry Kittredge continue to echo: "Those boys and girls will, in the future, do something in the way of strengthening the tie between your country and ours so far advanced by your generous idea."

Epilogue

The program began with a New England educator's judgment in 1948 that St. Paul's School must teach American boys about foreign cultures to prepare them for life in an increasingly international world. At the same time the Japanese had wanted to break out of centuries of insular isolation by learning about the powerful American democracy. These two independently shaped educational visions coincided. From the start both St. Paul's and Seikei leaders wanted to improve understanding between America and Japan. Then, dedicated and talented people worked hard to turn the visions into reality. Through the simple expedient of exposing young Japanese and American boys and girls to each other, they have succeeded beyond imagining.

What made this relationship work? How did people in two countries so separated by distance and history come to understand each other so well? How did enemies so viciously engaged in a brutal war join to make friends? How did it last through 50 years of changes in economies, personnel, technologies, academics, and demographics?

In 1932, before World War II, the new United States ambassador to Japan, Joseph C. Grew, spoke apt words to the American-Japan Society upon his arrival in Tokyo: "Sometimes our language—indeed all spoken languages—seems thin and superficial. We have to depend, in such cases, on a sort of x-ray language, which vibrates underneath the spoken words and is more often more effective than anything we can say. Your welcome justifies my hope that as we come to know each other better, this inaudible language, which perhaps extends less from mind to mind than from heart to heart, will prove to be an effective interpreter supplementing the often inadequate written or spoken word, whether in your tongue or mine...."

Both St. Paul's and Seikei are unique; neither is typical of its country's schools. Perhaps some subtle but profound silent language in each school's atmosphere extends from heart to heart. Seikei gives the highest quality education. So does SPS. Seikei graduates feel confident, superior, and unique. The same can be said for SPS graduates. Families of both SPS and Seikei want their children educated in the arts, humanities, literature, gaining knowledge for knowledge's sake. Both schools demand hard work and honesty.

Japanese society places importance on feeling what others think, restrained emotions, putting others at ease, being concerned about one's neighbors, working hard, and being honest. This reflects the cumulative effect of Japanese customs and social protocols—human relations with unwritten rules.

At St. Paul's it matters that others approve your behavior, that you understand others' feelings, and that emotions be controlled. Social norms are to be met—wear appropriate clothes, listen to others' opinions, respect the authority of teachers and coaches. The SPS culture values tradition, as does the Japanese culture. SPS students begin the day with chapel service; Seikei students gather in the auditorium to start the day in meditation in the Buddhist manner. The Japanese can understand the ceremony, manners, and sportsmanship that is so much a part of the SPS ethos. These common values perhaps formed a cultural bond that has held for 50 years.

This history may have emphasized the first three Seikei students to come to America in the aftermath of World War II. That is as it should be, for the 50th anniversary is a celebration of a beginning and of accomplishments. The first three have had vastly diverse characters and careers, exemplifying business, diplomatic and academic points of contact between the two countries.

Some of their successors will prove just as distinguished, just as courageous, just as accomplished. They, too, will have influence in the world. As the American and Japanese St. Paul's-Seikei scholars make their marks, their early education at the two great schools guide them. In return the students give back to the schools, as Makihara, Arima, and Shimizu have, with their talents, their friendship, and their loyalty.

After Kittredge, the lengthy administrations of Warren, Oates, and Clark presided over profound changes at St. Paul's School, and through them all the Seikei connection strengthened, adapted, and grew for half a century. Seikei principals such as Suzuki, Okuzumi, Yokote, Yokochi, and others sustained the exchanges throughout.

Alumni Association leaders like Kikuzo Tanioka, Richard D. Sawyer '48 and William Vogel '80 have supported the respective Japanese and American alumni and the contributions—not all financial—that they brought to the two schools. The relationship is strong. Its graduates are the rock of its foundation. In writing this I was struck again and again by their spirit, enthusiasm, and devotion.

The students are memorable. The teachers are memorable. Their connections are uncanny! In the 21st century new generations of students, administrators, and teachers are set to continue the St. Paul's-Seikei partnership. New ideas and technologies will create more dimensions to the relationship, some now unpredictable. Just as André Hurtgen and Satoru Nakajima succeeded Henry Kittredge, Mamoru Shimizu and William Oates, others will carry on with equal enthusiasm and dedication to their young charges and to Kittredge's original "generous idea."

Notes

The narrative is compiled from SPS and Seikei publications, SPS archives, personal files, oral and written recollections, responses to questionnaires, e-mail messages, and personal letters from people in the United States and Japan. I selected quotations, paraphrased descriptions of events, adapted material, and pieced together the history that was lived by the bright and interesting men and women who contributed.

In the following chapter notes, I have adopted the following shorthand:

"M. Shimizu files"—Mamoru Shimizu's file of correspondence between Seikei and St. Paul's School representatives from 1949 through 1955

Letters, notes, and memos from other personal files are also designated "files" with the writer's name (e.g., "Oates files").

Letters and e-mail I received are designated "letters" with the writer's name (for example, "Oates letters").

Student and teacher responses to questionnaires are identified with the writer's name, followed by "QR" (i.e., questionnaire response).

"SPS archives" are materials from one or another St. Paul's School archives or files.

Chapter 1

The early history of St. Paul's School is in August Heckscher's *St. Paul's: The Life of a New England School* (New York, Charles Scribner's Sons, 1980) and his *A Brief History of St. Paul's School 1856–1996* (Concord, N.H., St. Paul's School, 1996). The post-war school is described from my own memory.

Memorials to Henry Kittredge are in the *SPS Alumni Horae*, Spring 1967.

"It is hard enough...," *Annual Report of the Rector 1947–1948*.

"The geographical distribution of our boys...," *Annual Report of the Rector 1948–1949*. These reports seem to be the only direct documentation of Henry Kittredge's "idea."

There seem to be no surviving documents establishing how the first link between SPS and Seikei came about. William Oates remembered David Pyle's role at SPS. Mamoru Shimizu and Minoru Makihara confirmed Bishop Kenneth Viall's important role. Biographies in the Episcopal Church archives revealed that both Viall and Pyle lived in Tokyo before

World War II. This created a link for the first contact. Based on this link, I concluded that in 1949 Bishop Viall, then in Tokyo and Rev. Pyle in Concord must have known each other in pre-war Tokyo, probably communicated after the war and introduced the first Japanese student to SPS. A memorial to Pyle is in the SPS *Alumni Horae*, Autumn 1985.

General histories of World War II and William Manchester's *American Caesar: Douglas MacArthur 1880–1964* (New York, Little Brown and Company, 1978) describe the U.S. occupation of Japan. Makihara QR, Robert A. G. Monks interview, and Y. Shimizu interview provided information on the Makihara family in Tokyo.

The history of Seikei School is in *Seikei-St. Paul's 30th Anniversary 1949–1979* (Tokyo, 1979).

"Our class had been evacuated...," Bernard M. Makihara, "Friends," *Horae Scholasticae*, p. 45, February 1950.

Material in this chapter about Makihara's selection as the first Seikei student is in the M. Shimizu files and letters.

"Not knowing what was in store...," Kikuzo Tanioka, "Welcoming the Fiftieth Anniversary of the Educational Exchange," *Seikei-St. Paul's 50th Anniversary 1949–1999* (Tokyo, 1999).

"Sometime before Makihara-kun went...," Mamoru Shimizu, "How It Started—The Relationship Between St. Paul's School and Seikei," *Seikei-St. Paul's 35th Anniversary 1949–1984* (Tokyo, 1984).

"But, shortly after my arrival...," Makihara letter

"A few of us tried..., " Monks interview.

"When I arrived here...," Makihara speech, St. Paul's School, November 3, 1989. About Makihara at school—Monks interview and Makihara QR.

Makihara's Hugh Camp Cup Competition prize speech was originally printed in the SPS *Horae Scholasticae*, June 3, 1950.

"On the eve of our graduation...," Makihara letter.

"Although I stayed at SPS...," Makihara speech, St. Paul's School, November 3, 1989, SPS archives.

Chapter 2

The M. Shimizu files contain the letters from which are taken the quotations and the information about the negotiations and selection of the

Seikei scholars. General information about cost, immigration, and travel came from Y. Shimizu interview.

"My health certificate...," Tatsuo Arima, "From the Immigration Office," SPS *Horae Scholasticae*, June 1, 1953.

"I was accepted...," Tatsuo Arima, SPS *Alumni Horae*, p. 60, Summer 1978.

"Tatsuo Arima running hell for leather...," Nicholas Platt, ibid., p. 63.

"...[D]id so with a kind of meticulous slowness...," Arima letter. Arima's accomplishments are noted in St. Paul's School *Yearbook 1953* and Arima QR.

"I wanted to go to America...," Y. Shimizu interview. Information from several interviews with my classmate and friend Yoshiaki Shimizu provided details about his acceptance, arrival, and life at SPS. Details about his preparations are in M. Shimizu files. The "Japanese evening" was related in Griswold interview.

"Minoru has written... " M. Shimizu files.

"Speaking warmly of the students...," quoted in Kikuzo Tanioka, executive director of the Seikei Alumni Association, "Looking Back Over Thirty Years of Association Between St. Paul's School and Seikei," *Seikei-St. Paul's 30th Anniversary*, p. 31.

Matthew Warren's career is in August Heckscher's *A Brief History of St. Paul's School 1856–1996* and in "Matthew Madison Warren— Seventh Rector," SPS *Alumni Horae*, Spring 1986.

Chapter 3

"I was quite interested...," M. Shimizu files.

The letters between Warren and Seikei and the information about Hirai's acceptance are in the M. Shimizu files. Information about Hirai is in *The Seikei-St. Paul's Alumni Newsletter*, March 21, 1979; SPS *Yearbook 1957*, and Y. Shimizu interview.

The descriptions of the admissions process and change in the program are derived from SPS archives, Oates files, and Oates interview.

"All the flights from Tokyo...," Nakamura QR.

"There appears to be no end...," Warren Report quoted in August Heckscher's *A Brief History of St. Paul's School 1856–1996*, p.139.

"[P]ush a sturdy, parochial institution...," William A. Oates, *50th*

Anniversary Report, Harvard University, 1988, Oates files.

"All the Seikei students...," Satoru Nakajima letter.

"There was absolutely nothing..., " Arima letter.

"I immediately went out...," Iida QR.

"[L]ike a caged bird...," Akari Yamaguchi, "Encaged Birds," *Seikei-St. Paul's 40th Anniversary 1949–1989* (Tokyo, 1989), p. 45.

"Our experiences have taught us...," letter, Y. Shimizu, August 3, 1974, Oates file.

"The one unchangeable characteristic...," Oates files.

"Is there TV in Japan...," Hurtgen letter.

"On one occasion...," Terrence M. Walsh, "A Path to Friendship," SPS *Alumni Horae*, Spring 1979, p. 12.

"I have long wished...," ibid., p. 12.

"From this day on...," quoted in Walsh, ibid., p. 12.

"For 30 years...," William A. Oates, letter to SPS-Seikei alumni, October 3, 1978. *Seikei-St. Paul's 30th Anniversary 1949–1979*, p. 4.

Chapter 4

"The diversity was stunning...," Nobu QR.

"Looking back on that time...," Hall interview by Hurtgen.

"When we received an announcement...," McGowan letter.

The start of the SPS Japanese language program was described in Hurtgen interview, Oates interview, Okada interview, and Y. Shimizu interview.

"I knew that no rector had visited...," Oates files. The details of this visit and the meeting were in notes, memos, letters, and reports.

"We bring greetings...," Oates files.

"To start the discussion...," Oates files.

André Hurtgen described his sabbatical at Seikei in letters and interviews. His writings include "Two Schools, One Mind," for *Seikei-St. Paul's 35th Anniversary 1949–1984* (op. cit.) and "The Making of a Purposeful Society: A Year at Seikei Gakuen," SPS *Alumni Horae*, Summer 1984. A Nakajima letter told of Hurtgen at Seikei.

"I was struck time and time again...," Hurtgen, "The Making of a Purposeful Society: A Year at Seikei Gakuen," *SPS Alumni Horae*, Summer 1984.

"When the committee met...," Hurtgen letter.

"There were two girls and one boy... "McGowan letter.

"He was the principal resource...," Nakajima letter.

"We are not a Christian nation...," Nakajima letter.

"What differences there are...," André O. Hurtgen. "Two Schools, One Mind," *Seikei-St. Paul's Thirty-fifth Anniversary 1949–1984*.

The Shimano hiring and the Japanese language course descriptions are from Shimano interview with Hurtgen, SPS archives, and excerpts from Masatoshi Shimano and André Hurtgen, "The St. Paul's School Japanese Programs," *Journal of the Association of Teachers of Japanese*, Vol. 20, No. 1, April 1986.

"The answers we gave...," Oates letter.

"Thus we are opening windows...," Charles Clark, *Annual Report of the Rector, 1984–1985*, p. 15.

"They offered an essentially free...," Hurtgen letter.

"I take pleasure in expressing...," SPS archives.

"The students...have formed...," SPS archives.

"I believe we are going through...," SPS archives.

Chapter 5

1950 visit to Seikei, Barklay interview.

Recollections of the first Americans to attend Seikei, quotations from which are included this chapter, Nakajima letter.

Quotations about times at Seikei are taken from the letters and questionnaire responses of Loring McAlpin, Charles McKee, Elisabeth Bentel Carpenter, Tara McGowan Okada, Caroline Kenney, Joshua Brooks, Craig Sherman, and Timothy Ferriss. I adapted material from SPS archives.

"I was the first...," Stephen G. Vaskov, *Seikei 30th Anniversary*, reprinted from *The Seikei-St. Paul's Newsletter*, Vol. 1, No. 1 and quoted in Terrence M. Walsh, "A Path to Friendship," SPS *Alumni Horae*, p. 12, 1979.

"[W]ind-up toys...," Joseph Maybank IV, *Seikei PTA Newsletter*, 1981, quoted in Nakajima letters.

"Through the speeches...," Elisabeth Bentel, "First SPS-Seikei Student Reports on Life and Impressions of Japan," *SPS Pelican,* October 26, 1981, p. 2.

Chapter 6

"[P]rovide talented high school students...," *Advanced Studies Program 1999 Catalog,* SPS archives.

Advanced studies program graduates and Seikei teachers wrote letters from which quotations are taken. Hurtgen letters and interviews provided much material. Jeff Bradley and André Hurtgen furnished background and statistics.

"All of Takahiro's successors...," Hurtgen letter.

Chapter 7

"There are many people...," Makihara, "Announcing the Establishment of the SPS Club of Japan," March 1991, SPS archives. The narrative of the alumni activity is compiled from correspondence, minutes, and announcements in SPS archives.

"As I visited the Chapel...," Y. Shimizu, "Reflection on a Life in America," *Seikei-St. Paul's 40th Anniversary 1949–1989,* p. 29.

"What interests me most...," *SPS Pelican,* October 24, 1997.

The Anderson's visit to Seikei, reported in "Seikei-SPS Club Honors Andersons," *SPS Today,* Vol. 4, No. 2, July 1998.

"Mr. Kitajima, I want to thank you...," author's notes.

"For your honoring him...," author's notes.

"The ceremony was simple...," Oates interview.

"[L]avish and elegant...," Hurtgen letter.

The description of the SPS 50th anniversary celebration, chapel service, symposium and dinner, author's notes.

"[I]s more important now...," Quoted in James Flannigan, "Premier's Visit at Critical Time for Japan, U.S.," *Los Angeles Times,* May 2, 1999.

"Sir Rector...," Anderson files.

Chapter 8

"Understanding a foreign culture...," André Hurtgen, "How Seikei Students Expanded My World," *Seikei-St. Paul's 50th Anniversary Book, 1999*.

"St. Paul's and Seikei celebrate...," Clark, *Annual Report of the Rector, 1984–1985*, p. 15.

"I believe that those three boys...," M. Shimizu files.

"The single-most influential individual...," Akira Iriye, "Edwin O. Reischauer," *American National Biography* (New York, Oxford University Press, 1999).

Information on Makihara is compiled from Makihara QR, Monks interview, magazine and newspaper articles, the Seikei anniversary books, and the *Alumni Horae*. A brief history of the Mitsubishi companies was in *Business Week*, March 15, 1999, and Mark Weston, *Giants of Japan* (New York, Kodansha America, Inc., 1999).

"The most famous of Japanese...," *New York Times*, April 12, 1992.

"My background is very nontraditional...," ibid.

"[G]reatest achievement...," *Far Eastern Economic Review*, October 3, 1996.

The remarks by Arima and Platt were quoted in "Involved in the Process of History," SPS *Alumni Horae*, Summer 1978, p. 60, et. seq. Information on Arima is compiled from *1997 Ferguson Scholar's Book*, Arima QR, Platt interview, Oates letter, and Arima, "Random Recollections of My Arrival at St. Paul's," Seikei Alumni Association, *Seikei-St.Paul's 50th Anniversary 1949–1989*.

The material on Yoshiaki Shimizu was compiled from Y. Shimizu interviews, correspondence with St. Paul's School in SPS archives, his writings in Seikei anniversary books, and the *Alumni Horae*.

The Daimyo exhibit is described in National Gallery of Art Archives and Yoshiaki Shimizu, *Japan, The Shaping of Daimyo Culture, 1185–1868* (Washington, 1988).

Material on the careers of Japanese and American SPS graduates and ASP students was taken from their letters and questionnaire responses.

"I elected to use my bicultural educational experience...," Suzuki, "U.S.-Japan Communications," Seikei Alumni Assoctation, *Seikei-St.Paul's 40th Anniversary 1949–1989*.

"I sat in and found...," Sherman, "A Foundation for Mutual

Understanding," Seikei Alumni Association, *Seikei-St.Paul's 50th Anniversary 1949–1999*.

"It's a scary thought...," Kitano (nee Nishikawa), "A Turning Point in My Life," Seikei Alumni Association. Ibid., *1949–1999*.

"At my request...," Oates letter.

Epilogue

"Sometimes our language...," Joseph C. Grew, *Ten Years in Japan* (New York, Simon & Schuster, 1944), p. 22.

Bibliography

Books

American National Biography (New York: Oxford University Press, 1999).

Costello, John. *The Pacific War* (New York, William Morrow & Co., 1982).

Grew, Joseph C. *Ten Years in Japan* (New York: Simon & Schuster, 1944).

Heckscher, August. *St. Paul's: The Life of a New England School* (New York: Charles Scribner's Sons, 1980).

Heckscher, August. *A Brief History of St. Paul's School 1856–1996* (Concord, N.H.: St. Paul's School, 1996).

Japan Travel Bureau, Inc. *A Look into Japan* (1984).

Manchester, William. *American Caesar: Douglas MacArthur* (New York, Little Brown and Company, 1978).

Seikei Alumni Association. *Seikei-St.Paul's 30th Anniversary 1949–1979* (Tokyo, 1979).

Seikei Alumni Association. *Seikei-St.Paul's 35th Anniversary 1949–1984* (Tokyo, 1984).

Seikei Alumni Association. *Seikei-St.Paul's 40th Anniversary 1949–1989* (Tokyo, 1989).

Seikei Alumni Association. *Seikei-St.Paul's 50th Anniversary 1949–1999* (Tokyo, 1999).

Seikei Junior High School, Senior High School. *2000 Guide* (Tokyo, 1999).

St. Paul's School. *Advanced Studies Program, 1999, Catalogue.*

St. Paul's School. Advanced Studies Program, *Newsletter*, March 1998.

St. Paul's School. *Alumni Horae.*

St. Paul's School. *Annual Report of the Rector*, 1948–1985.

St. Paul's School. *Course Descriptions, 1999–2000.*

St. Paul's School. *The Record and Annual Support.*

St. Paul's School Yearbooks, 1950–1999.

Periodicals

The Seikei-St. Paul's Alumni Newsletter, March 21, 1979.

St. Paul's School. *Alumni Horae:*

"Henry Crocker Kittredge," Spring 1967, p. 3.

"Pure Juice of the Cape Cod Grape," Spring 1967, p. 10.

"Henry Kittredge as Housemaster, Teacher, Citizen," Spring 1967, p. 12.

"Matthew Madison Warren—Seventh Rector," Spring 1986.

"Memorials, The Reverend David McAlpin Pyle," Autumn 1985, p. 148.

"Francis Vernon Lloyd, Jr., 1908–1993," Spring 1993.

St. Paul's School Today

"Seikei-SPS Club Honors Andersons," July 1998.

St. Paul's School *The Pelican.*

Articles

Arima, Tatsuo. "From the Immigration Office," *SPS Horae Scholasticae*, June 1, 1953.

——— and Nicholas Platt. "Involved in the Process of History," *SPS Alumni Horae*, Summer 1978.

Bentel, Elisabeth. "First SPS-Seikei Student Reports on Life and Impressions of Japan," *The Pelican*, October 26, 1981.

———. "Elisabeth Bentel Writes from Japan," *The Pelican*, December 7, 1981.

———. "Bentel: New Year's in Japan," *The Pelican*, March 8, 1982.

———. "Foreign Correspondent Bentel Signs Off," *The Pelican*, May 24, 1982.

Bremner, Brian. "The President Has a Will—But No Way," *Business Week*, March 15, 1999.

Brown, Mich. "Artist of the Issue Karen Shimizu Tells All," *SPS Pelican*, October 24, 1997.

Flannigan, James. "Premier's Visit at Critical Time for Japan, U. S.," *Los Angeles Times*, May 2, 1999.

Hurtgen, André O. "The Making of a Purposeful Society: A Year at Seikei Gakuen," *Alumni Horae*, Summer 1984.

———."Two Schools, One Mind," *Seikei-St. Paul's 35th Anniversary 1949–1984* (Tokyo, 1984).

———. "Languages and Internationalism at St. Paul's School," *Alumni Horae*, Autumn 1988.

———. "How Japanese Students Expanded My World," *Seikei-St. Paul's 50th Anniversary 1949–1999* (Tokyo, 1999).

Makihara, B. Minoru. "Friends," *SPS Horae Scholasticae*, February 1950.

———. "The Hen," *SPS Horae Scholasticae*, March 1950.

McKee, Charles. "Correspondent from Japan: Lesson 1," *The Pelican*, February 22, 1982.

"Minoru Makihara," *Far Eastern Economic Review*, Hong Kong, October 3, 1996.

Sanger, David E. "Unusual Path to the Top at Mitsubishi," *The New York Times*, April 13, 1992.

"Seikei-St. Paul's Relations: 40 Year Friendship Honored," *The Pelican*, November 7, 1989.

Shimano, Masatoshi and André Hurtgen. "The St. Paul's School Japanese Programs," *Journal of the Association of Teachers of Japanese*, Vol. 20, No. 1, April 1986.

"SPS-Seikei 40th Anniversary," *Alumni Horae*, 1989.

Tanioka, Kikuzo. "Looking Back Over Thirty Years of Association Between St. Paul's School and Seikei," *Seikei-St. Paul's 30th Anniversary 1949–1979* (Tokyo, 1979), p. 31.

Walsh, Terrence M. "A Path to Friendship," *Alumni Horae*, April 1980.

Further Reading

Arima, Tatsuo. "The Inner Landscape of Japanese Culture: A Personal Reflection," Hoover Institution, Stanford University; speech delivered at the Reischauer Institute, Harvard University, November 23, 1987.

———. The Failure of Freedom: A Portrait of Modern Japanese Intellectuals (Cambridge, Mass.: Harvard University Press, 1969).

Buckley, Roger. *US–Japan Alliance Diplomacy 1945–1990* (Cambridge University Press, 1995). [A diplomatic history]

Hosokawa, William K. *Nisei: The Quiet Americans* (New York: William Morrow & Co., 1969). [The history of the Japanese people in America]

Makihara, B. Minoru. Foreword to Robert A. G Monks and Nell Minow, *Watching the Watchers: Corporate Governance for the 21st Century*, (Cambridge, Mass.: Blackwell Publishers, 1996).

O'Toole, Kathleen. "Profile, John Taylor," *Magazine of the Stanford Alumni Association,* July/August 1998. [Compares Japanese and American College students]

Reischauer, Edwin O. and Marius B. Jansen. *The Japanese Today* (Cambridge, Mass.: Harvard University Press, 1995).

Rockefeller, John D. III. Preface to *Report on the Exhibition of Japanese Painting and Sculpture, January–December 1953* (Tokyo, 1954).

Schonberger, Howard B. *Aftermath of War: Americans and the Remaking of Japan 1945–1952* (Kent, Oh.: Kent State University Press, 1989). [A history]

Shimizu, Yoshiaki. *Japan, The Shaping of Daimyo Culture, 1185–1868* (Washington, D.C.: National Gallery of Art, 1988). [Exhibition catalogue with extensive history and commentary]

———. "Japan in Museums," Speech delivered at symposium at the Freer Gallery of Art, Smithsonian Institution, Washington, D.C., October 3, 1998.

———. "Chasing the Moon," *SPS Horae Scholasticae, 1954–55.* [Williamson Prize–winning essay]

———. "Japanese Painting from the Collection of J. D. Price" (University of Kansas, 1967).

———. "Japanese Ink Paintings" (Princeton University Press, 1976).

Weston, Mark. *Giants of Japan: The Lives of Japan's Most Influential Men and Women* (New York; Kodansha American, Inc., 1999).

Appendix A

Hugh Camp Cup Competition
St. Paul's School *Horae Scholasticae*
June 3, 1950

By B. Minoru Makihara, SPS '50

Prize Speech

Jefferson said that all men are created equal and I sincerely believe that all men should be given equal opportunities in their lives, but does this mean that you and I are identical, that a Japanese boy would be doing the same things that you would be doing? No. All men are created equal but they are not the same.

Human beings are to some extent modified by the circumstances by which they live. Let me illustrate this with a very simple example. If I were now in Japan, what would I be doing? First of all I wouldn't wear the same clothes as I do here. I would be wearing a black cape and a torn black cap; I would be wearing wooden clogs instead of these shoes; and I would have a filthy towel dangling from my belt. Why do Japanese students dress like this? There are several reasons. There are economic reasons: They do not have enough money to buy new clothes. There are practical reasons: It is damp and hot in Japan, so it is quite pleasant to wear wooden clogs. But there is something more than that. As a result of their long contact with Asiatic mysticism and Buddhism, Japanese students have a great affinity for philosophy in general. They like to think in abstract terms, and so there is a tendency among the students to show externally that they do not care about material things. Thus we see that a Japanese student would have a different way of thinking compared with you, the boys of St. Paul's School. We Japanese live on a small island in the Far East; we have 2,000-year-old history behind us, and we are products of this background. I do not mean that some nations are superior to others because of different backgrounds. I do not mean that at all. What I want to say is that we Japanese have a different way of thinking, a different psychology.

Too often mistakes have been made because people have failed to recognize this fact. And this same error has been made over and over again by many sincere people. For instance, you may believe in the rightness of the American form of democracy. But can you force that same form onto other countries? This form of democracy may be the best form for this country. But from that, does it follow that this form of democracy will be the best for all nations? Not necessarily. You must understand that different nations will show different reactions, even when they are confronted with the same problems. You must take into account what those people are thinking about, their history, and the circumstances in which they live.

For example, there are some people who criticize the Chinese Reds for being anti-democratic, just because the Reds do not have the same form of government that we do. But I wonder how such a comparison can be drawn between America and China, a country that has long been dominated by feudal landlords, and whose population consists largely of peasants who are totally uneducated. In such a country, what kind of a government could be better than one that gives land to the peasants and tries to lead them to a higher standard of living?

America has failed in many instances because there were some people who were incapable of interpreting facts; and I especially direct this criticism towards America, because a mistake made by America will be more damaging than a mistake made by other countries.

I believe that from among the boys of this school we shall see diplomats, politicians, and statesmen appear, and I believe that all of you will become active members of this democratic society. Therefore I ask you again, please try to understand the different backgrounds of different nations. You may boast that you are open-minded, that you are unprejudiced, and that you are ready to accept facts, but that is not enough. If you are unable to collect facts, select them, and interpret them correctly, it is as bad as being prejudiced. You may accept the fact that a Japanese student looks different, but if you cannot look beyond his appearance and realize its significance, your acceptance of it is meaningless.

I am here at St. Paul's School, trying to know more about America, and there are millions of students in Asia who want to learn more about this country. Let us do our best to understand each other. It will be a hard task. We shall have to know each other's history and cultural backgrounds. But it is only in this way that we are going to be drawn together, because "all men are created equal, but they are not the same."

Appendix B

SPS-SEIKEI 1949–1999
Japanese Students at St. Paul's	*At SPS*

Bernard Minoru Makihara	1949–50
Tatsuo Arima	1951–53
Yoshiaki Shimizu	1953–55
Toshimichi Hirai (d. 1998)	1955–57
Motoi Okubo	1957–59
Hachiro Nakamura	1959–61
Yoshiharu Akabane	1961–63
Junji Shioda (d. 1989)	1963–65
Kaoruhiko Suzuki	1965–67
Eijiro Yamauchi	1967–69
Kiyoshi Matsumi Kikyo	1969–71
Kaoru Iida (m. Yamauchi)	1972–75
Amy Yoshiko Nobu	1975–78
Makoto Tokutomi	1976–79
Toshikazu Yamashita	1977–78
Kaori Kitazawa (d. 1982)	1978–81
Yoichi Hiraki	1979–81
Haruki Minaki	1979–81
Hiroko Yamashita	1980–81
Akiko Higaki	1981–84
Miki Tanaka	1982–84
Rika Hayashi	1983–86
Junko Watanabe	1984–86
Akari Yamaguchi	1986–89
Yoko Nishikawa	1987–90
Aya Nakazato	1988–91
Michiyuki Nagasawa	1989–91

Daishi Yamada	1989–92
Hana Sugimoto	1990–92
Leon Ochiai	1991–94
Fumi Akiyama	1992–94
Aki Kawashima	1993–95
Ayako Kubota	1994–97
Shunsuke Okano	1995–97
Hisako Watanabe	1996–98
Masayuki Yuda	1997–00
Takeshi Morita	1998–01
Kaoru Chikushi	1999–01

Appendix C

SPS-SEIKEI 1949–1999
American Students at Seikei

	At Seikei	SPS Class
Stephen G. Vaskov	March–May 1976	1976
Loring R. McAlpin	January–March 1978	1978
Joseph Maybank IV	January–July 1981	1980
M. Elisabeth Bentel (m. Carpenter)	1981–82	1983
Charles D. McKee, Jr.	1981–82	1983
Kimball P. Collins	1982	1982
Tara McGowan (m. Okada)	1982–83	1984
John C. Euler	1983–84	1985
Craig D. Sherman	1984–85	1985
Joshua H. Brooks	1986–87	1986
Joshua B. Nickerson	1987–88	1987
Eugene Sung	June–July 1989	1991

Jason M. Dahlstrom	1990–91	1992
Tanya E. Wilcox	1990–91	1992
Caroline E. Kenney	1990–91	1990
Julian Jiro Wimbush	September–January 1991	1990
Brian A. Smith	1992–93	1994
Timothy C. Ferriss	1993–94	1995
Stephanie Y. Ho	January–March 1995	1995
Everett K. Sands	January–March 1995	1995
Colin McLear	January–March 1995	1996
Kang Kim	January–March 1999	1999
Syung Youn Nam	January–July 1999	1999
Jun ho Bae	April–July 1999	1999

Appendix D

Visiting Japanese Teachers

Mr. Takahiro Hiraoka	1985
Mr. Satoru Nakajima	1986
Mr. Kiyoshi Kuroki	1987
Mr. Tsuneharu & Mrs. Aiko Kubota	1988
Mr. Hisao & Mrs. Takako Minami	1989
Mr. Tadaaki Shimizu	1990
Mr. Akihiko Yoshida	1991
Ms. Sumiko Nakamura	1992
Mr. Koichi Nihei	1993
Ms. Rumiko Okada	1994
Ms. Sayaka Atobe	1995
Mr. Yoshiharu Irino	1996
Ms. Hiromi Takahashi	1997

Ms. Michiko Yamato   1998
Mr. Mitsuru Nishihara   1999

Appendix E

ST.PAUL'S-SEIKEI Prize Recipients

The St. Paul's-Seikei Prize is awarded annually by the language department to a high-achieving student who encouraged or participated in the exchange program. The recipients have been:

1990	Julian J. Wimbush
1991	Clay C-C. Wang
1992	Tanya E. Wilcox
1993	Dana A. Remus
1994	Brian A. Smith
1995	Timothy C. Ferriss
1996	Argyro P. Caminis and Angus R. Maclaurin
1997	Ma-lung Chen and Li-Ting Wang
1998	Piyajit Phanaphat
1999	Syung Youn Nam

Appendix F
SPS Awards Recipients

Seikei Scholars at SPS have received impressive academic honors— all the more impressive for working in a second language.

Minoru Ben Makihara '50	Hugh Camp Cup (public speaking); *Magna cum laude*
Tatsuo Arima '53	Ferguson Scholarship; *Magna cum laude*
Yoshiaki Shimizu '55	Williamson Medal (essay) S. Ellesworth Greenley Prize (Art) Hugh Camp Cup (public speaking); *Cum laude*
Toshimichi Hirai '57	*Magna cum laude*
Hachiro Nakamura '61	*Cum laude*
Yoshiharu Akabane '63	*Cum laude*
Kaoruhiko Suzuki '67	*Magna cum laude* SPS Honor Scholarship (exceptional scholarship)
Amy Yoshiko Nobu '78	*Cum laude*
Kaori Kitazawa '81	*Magna cum laude* Rector's Award SPS Honor Scholarship
Miki Tanaka '84	*Cum laude*
Rika Hayashi '86	Keiser Prize (music)
Junko Watanabe '86	*Magna cum laude* John Hargate Medal (highest rank in math) Joseph Howland Coit Medal (geometry)

Akari Yamaguchi '89	*Summa cum laude* John Hargate Medal (two years) Joseph Howland Coit Medal
Yoko Nishikawa '90	*Cum laude* Keiser Prize (music performance and composition, two years) Howe Prize (interest in music) Rector's Award
Michiyuki Nagasawa '91	*Summa cum laude*
Hana Sugimoto '92	*Cum laude*
Fumi Akiyama '94	*Cum laude* Tennis Award
Ayako Kubota '97	*Magna cum laude* Giles Prize (band)
Sunsuke Okano '97	Schlager Prize for Valor
Hisako Watanabe '98	*Magna cum laude*

Photo Credits

P. 5 Y. Shimizu; P. 6 M. Barwell; P. 9 SPS; P. 14 SPS; P. 16 T. Hiraoka; P. 17 SPS; P. 19 SPS; P. 21 SPS; P. 25 SPS; P. 30 Y. Shimizu; P. 34 SPS; P. 36 Y. Shimizu; P. 37 SPS; P. 39 Y. Shimizu; P. 42 SPS; P. 49 SPS; P. 54 L. Ochiai; P. 55 Y. Nichikawa and M. Nagasawa; P. 58 S. Nakajima; P. 61 SPS; P. 64 W. Oates; P. 65 W. Oates; P. 68 SPS; P. 69 A. Hurtgen; P. 75 S. Nakajima; P. 78 Seikei; P. 80 C. Kenney; P. 81 L. McAlpin; P. 83 Seikei; P. 85 S. Nakajima; P. 86 S. Nakajima; P. 87 S. Nakajima; P. 89 S. Nakajima; P. 90 T. Ferriss; P. 91 S. Nakajima; P. 92 C. Kenney; P. 94 M. Yamato; P. 97 A. Hurtgen; P. 98 A. Hurtgen; P. 100 M. Yamato; P. 101 A. Hurtgen; P. 110 J. Wimbush and SPS; P. 112 S. Nakajima; P. 111 Consul General of Japan; P. 114 D. Dana; P. 116 Y. Shimizu; P. 125 A. Nobu; P. 128 Y. Nichikawa and E. Carpenter

David T. Dana III graduated from St. Paul's *cum laude* in 1955. A member of the Cadmean and Concordian literary societies, he won the Isthmian Medal and made his first appearance in print with a short story in the *Horae Scholasticae*. He earned honors in history at Princeton and an award for his thesis, *The Marshall Mission to China 1945-47*, then took a law degree from Yale in 1962. After serving in the Marine Corps, Mr. Dana practiced law, first in Delaware, then in California for a quarter of a century. Upon retiring, he returned to the discipline of history. He has edited a travel journal of the 1850s and published an eye-witness account of the Civil War naval engagement at Mobile Bay, and is now beginning a study of America's 19th-century China Trade. Formerly an adjunct professor at Western State University College of Law, he has published in the California State Bar Journal and the Western State University Law Review and has reviewed draft legal codes for new East European democracies under auspices of the American Bar Association. Mr. Dana has served as president of his local Princeton Alumni Club, Newport Balboa Rotary Club Foundation and Bay Broadcasters Toastmasters Club. Born in Massachusetts and a second-generation SPS graduate, Mr. Dana now lives in Carlsbad, California, with his wife of 35 years, Marcie. They have two children and a grandson.

A Generous Idea; St. Paul's School and Seikei Gakuen was designed by Constance D. Dillman, Tom Suzuki, Inc., Falls Church, VA. The text is set in Sabon and Franklin Gothic. The first edition was printed on 70 Finch Opaque Cream Smooth by Courier Westford Inc. of Westford, MA.

Letter of Appreciation
To
St. Paul's School

August 15, 1984

St. Paul's School, having energetically practiced an educational exchange program with the Seikei Upper Secondary School since 1949, has played a significant role in promoting mutual understanding between Japan and the United States of America.

On this auspicious occasion of the thirty-fifth anniversary of the program, I take pleasure in expressing my profound appreciation to this eminent American school for the efforts and contributions it has rendered over the years for the strengthening of friendly relations between our two countries.

Shintaro Abe
Minister for Foreign Affairs
of Japan